The BEST Angel STORIES 2015

The BEST
Angel STORIES
2015

Angels
ON EARTH

New York

The Best Angel Stories 2015

Published by Guideposts Books & Inspirational Media
110 William Street
New York, New York 10038
Guideposts.org

Acknowledgments

Every attempt has been made to credit the sources of copyrighted material used in this book. If any such acknowledgment has been inadvertently omitted or miscredited, receipt of such information would be appreciated.

"A Big Fish Came" is reprinted from *Fast Lane to Heaven* by Ned Dougherty with permission from Hampton Roads. Copyright © 2001 by Ned Dougherty. All rights reserved.

"A Guy Named Andy" by Timothy J. Burt from *Heaven Touching Earth* compiled by James Stuart Bell is used by permission from Bethany House Publishers, a division of Baker Publishing Group. Copyright © 2014 by James Stuart Bell. All rights reserved.

"A Visitation from an Angel" is reprinted from *A Glimpse of Heaven* by Carla Wills-Brandon with permission from White Crow Books. Copyright © by 2012 Carla Wills-Brandon. All rights reserved.

"Angels Are Watching Over Me" by Alice M. McGhee from *Heaven Touching Earth* compiled by James Stuart Bell is used by permission from Bethany House Publishers, a division of Baker Publishing Group. Copyright © 2014 by James Stuart Bell. All rights reserved.

"Angel in a White Suit" by Shawn Bolz is reprinted from *Angel Stories* by Jonathan Nixon with permission from Charisma House. Copyright © 2014 by Jonathan Nixon. All rights reserved.

"Angel in the Mirror" by Sally Edwards Danley from *Heaven Touching Earth* compiled by James Stuart Bell is used by permission from Bethany House Publishers, a division of Baker Publishing Group. Copyright © 2014 by James Stuart Bell. All rights reserved.

"Buddy's Welcome Home" by Wanda Rosseland originally appeared in the July/August 2014 issue of *Angels on Earth* and is used by permission of the author. Copyright © 2014 by Wanda Rosseland. All rights reserved.

"Great Aunt Antoinette's Angels" is reprinted from *A Glimpse of Heaven* by Carla Wills-Brandon with permission from White Crow Books. Copyright © 2012 by Carla Wills-Brandon. All rights reserved.

"Hand of an Angel" by Cindy Huron is reprinted from *A Book of Miracles* by Dr. Bernie Siegel with permission from New World Library. Copyright © 2011 by Bernie S. Siegel. All rights reserved.

"It Sparked!" by Elizabeth A. Nixon is reprinted from *Angel Stories* by Jonathan Nixon with permission from Charisma House. Copyright © 2014 by Jonathan Nixon. All rights reserved.

"No Longer Abandoned" by Judy Hampton from *Heaven Touching Earth* compiled by James Stuart Bell is used by permission from Bethany House Publishers, a division of Baker Publishing Group. Copyright © 2014 by James Stuart Bell. All rights reserved.

"Penniless in Bangkok" by Scoti Springfield Domeij from *Heaven Touching Earth* compiled by James Stuart Bell is used by permission from Bethany House Publishers, a division of Baker Publishing Group. Copyright © 2014 by James Stuart Bell. All rights reserved.

"The Angel in the Flannel Shirt" by Jeannine Rodriguez-Everard is reprinted from *Angel Stories* by Jonathan Nixon with permission from Charisma House. Copyright © 2014 by Jonathan Nixon. All rights reserved.

"The Lady of the Light" is reprinted from *Fast Lane to Heaven* by Ned Dougherty with permission from Hampton Roads. Copyright © 2001 by Ned Dougherty. All rights reserved.

"The Midnight Traveler" by Linda Howton, as told to Joyce Gatton from *Heaven Touching Earth* compiled by James Stuart Bell is used by permission from Bethany House Publishers, a division of Baker Publishing Group. Copyright © 2014 by James Stuart Bell. All rights reserved.

"The Rescue Angel" by Randy DeMain is reprinted from *Angel Stories* by Jonathan Nixon with permission from Charisma House. Copyright © 2014 by Jonathan Nixon. All rights reserved.

"The Travel Agent Angel" by Doug Addison is reprinted from *Angel Stories* by Jonathan Nixon with permission from Charisma House. Copyright © 2014 by Jonathan Nixon. All rights reserved.

Scripture quotations marked (KJV) are taken from the King James Version of the Bible.

Scripture quotations marked (NIV) are taken from *The Holy Bible, New International Version*. Copyright © 1973, 1978, 1984, 2011 by Biblica, Inc. Used by permission of Zondervan. All rights reserved worldwide. www.zondervan.com

Illustration on page 1 is © 2013 by Tristan Elwell. All rights reserved. Illustration on page 49 is © 2014 by Sylvie Thamsir. All rights reserved. Illustration on page 89 is © 2014 by Andrea Wicklund. All rights reserved. Illustration on page 129 is © 2013 by Joe Taylor. All rights reserved. Illustration on page 173 is © 2014 by Dan Craig. All rights reserved. Illustration on page 203 is © 2014 by Chris Koehler. All rights reserved. Illustration on page 235 is © 2012 by Tristan Elwell. All rights reserved. Illustration on page 261 is © 2012 by Dan Craig. All rights reserved.

Cover and interior design by Müllerhaus
Cover and interior art Copyright © 2014 by Dan Craig
Typesetting by Aptara

Printed and bound in the United States of America
10 9 8 7 6 5 4 3 2 1

Contents

Chapter 2
Safe in Their Care
49

Chapter 3
Angels in Disguise
89

Introduction

HOW DO YOU FACT-CHECK an angel story? That's what I wanted to know back when I was researching my first story for *Angels on Earth*, a magazine Guideposts launched in 1995 to share people's stories about the experience that changed their life—the moment they met an angel.

And although it feels as quick as the flutter of an angel's wing, this year *Angels on Earth* is celebrating its twentieth anniversary. In that time, meeting and working daily with people who have been touched by an angel, I've learned that checking the facts is only one part of an editor's role. We listen for the truth of each story, and then help each person tell the experience with all of its unique detail so that it comes to life in your mind's eye, as real as if you'd seen and heard and felt it yourself.

The Best Angel Stories 2015 is our all-new, annual collection that features the stand-out stories of the year showing how God and His angels watch over us. It includes best-loved stories from this year's *Angels on Earth* magazine, as well as over a dozen never before published stories and enduring classics from our twenty-year history, like "May Wind," my favorite story from our premiere issue. Florence B. Smith worried that her handicapped son would never grasp the concept of God—until angels flew in through the billowing curtains of his bedroom window.

You'll meet earth angels and heavenly angels, and some that will leave you wondering to which category they belong. You'll read of an encounter with the voice of an angel, a bald African-American angel, an average-looking-Joe kind of angel, a warm-as-a-blanket angel, a baking angel, an angel with paws, even a pod of angels.

This book delivers a feast of remarkable true accounts, each one uplifting and joyous. It is filled with amazing rescues, inexplicable protection, immeasurable reassurance, answers that come in dreams and visions, mysterious comfort from beyond, and more! These stories stretch the boundaries of the human imagination and connect us in those inexplicable experiences we all share.

You'll discover that each angel is like no other, as unique as the individual who needs protection or comfort, and love, always love. "You are loved" is the message of all angels, no matter what form they take. That message is the theme running throughout this book, and is at the heart of every story here. Every true story.

How do we know the truth of an angel experience? After twenty years, I know that sometimes the heart is the only reliable source.

I'd love to hear your angel story. Please send it to me at *Angels on Earth*, 110 William Street, New York, New York, 10038 or e-mail us at submissions@angelsonearth.org.

—COLLEEN HUGHES
Angels on Earth Editor-in-Chief

The BEST Angel STORIES 2015

CHAPTER 1

Guarded by Angels

He will cover you with his feathers,

and under his wings you will find refuge . . . .

For he will command his angels concerning you

to guard you in all your ways;

they will lift you up in their hands,

so that you will not strike your foot against a stone.

—PSALM 91:4, 11–12 (NIV)

Protected
Marcus Sams

MR. RESPONSIBLE. THAT'S ME. My friends liked to joke about it, but I took things seriously. That's why I was the one driving my three friends back to school after play practice. The day was drizzly, so I was extra careful on I-35. I kept my eyes on the road, except for a quick glance in the rearview mirror. "Lauren!" I said. "Put on your seat belt!"

Lauren was sprawled sideways across the backseat with her foot on Matt's knee. "We're almost to the school, Marcus," she said. "I want to keep my ankle elevated. I think I might have sprained it on stage."

"That's no good reason to take chances," I said. "You never know what can happen on the interstate."

I looked at Molly beside me in the passenger seat of my mom's SUV. At least her seat belt was on.

Lauren sighed and pulled out the seat belt. I hated to sound like a nag, but safety was important. I remembered back to my sixteenth birthday—the same day I took my driver's test. Mom was so proud when I flashed her my new ID in the driveway, but not so proud she didn't give me a lecture. "Driving is a big responsibility," she said. "You and your friends are precious cargo."

"I know, Mom," I said.

Hadn't I proved myself by acing my driving test? What else did I need to be safe? Mom pulled something out of her pocket. "I trust you'll always drive carefully," she said. "But I want you to slip this clip on your visor for extra protection."

She dropped a little round clip into my hand. It was a guardian angel. *Mothers,* I thought.

As we neared our exit on I-35, I glanced up at the clip still fastened on the visor. I hadn't had any need for a guardian angel yet—not with my careful driving—but it didn't hurt to have it. It was like I told Lauren about the seat belt. You never knew what can happen on the interstate.

I moved into the next lane and turned on my right signal. The fifteenth street exit was coming up. In a few minutes we'd be back in the school parking lot.

I slowed down to take the sharp curve. But when I turned the wheel the SUV hydroplaned. I hit the brakes. We slid and swerved back and forth over the road. "It's okay!" I said as calmly as I could. "It's okay!"

We fishtailed sharply to the right. I'd practiced spinning out of control with my dad in empty parking lots so I'd be prepared for something like this. Now was time to put those lessons into effect. I gripped the steering wheel tight and turned the wheels hard in the direction of the spin.

But a slippery interstate wasn't like an empty parking lot. Instead of slowing down, the car spun faster. The tires on one side ran over the curb and dropped into a drainage ditch. The whole SUV tilted and flipped. My friends screamed. My door slammed into the ground. Then we were upside down. Then the passenger side hit the ground. We tumbled down the grassy slope, over and over, like a wooden block tossed down a hill. The car was filled with the sound of crunching metal and shattering glass. My passengers went silent in shock.

We must have rolled over eight or nine times. When we finally stopped, the driver's side lay on the grass and the front of the car faced the highway. Glass covered the dashboard and seats like sharp confetti. My heart pounded in my chest. I twisted in my seat. "Is everyone okay?" I croaked.

Lauren and Molly hung suspended in their seat belts on the passenger side. Matt, like me, was on the side nearest the ground.

"Yes," Molly whispered.

"I seem to be," said Lauren.

"What's that smell?" asked Matt.

Burnt rubber? Gasoline? All I knew was, we shouldn't be in this car a minute longer. With shaking hands I got my seat belt unbuckled. Matt and I stood up. I held Molly around her waist as she unbuckled her seat belt while Matt helped Lauren. But when we tried to get out, the passenger-side doors were jammed. The jagged glass made the windows too dangerous to try to climb out.

I don't know what to do, I thought. *How do we get out of here?*

I poked my head out the window next to Molly hoping—praying—there was someone outside to help. *Whoa!* Just outside the car, as if he'd been waiting for me, stood one of the biggest men I'd ever seen. He was African American and bald, maybe in his late thirties, wearing jeans and a white T-shirt. He looked about the size of an NFL linebacker—only taller.

"You kids all right?" he asked in a deep baritone.

"We're okay, but we can't get out."

"Allow me," he said.

He reached into the car, put his hands under Lauren's armpits, and plucked her up as if she were a toddler. He pulled her gently through the window, avoiding all the broken glass, and set her on the grass. Molly spread out her arms and he lifted her out. Next came Matt. Then it was my turn.

I'm about five-feet-eleven, but I felt like a baby when he picked me up in his hands the size of oven mitts. When I stood on the ground outside of the car I came up to his chest. He must have been seven feet tall.

"You're going to be okay," he said.

The girls rushed me and Matt for a hug, and I heard sirens coming our way. I turned to thank our rescuer, but he was gone.

"How could a man that size disappear so fast?" I said, looking up and down the service road for a clue. I didn't even see a car that might have been his.

A couple of firefighters jogged up and asked if we were all right. "A stranger pulled us out of the car," I said. "Right before you pulled up."

The firemen just looked at each other. "But we saw you climbing out of the car when we drove up. There was no one else here."

Maybe I was more shaken by the crash than I thought. But we didn't *all* imagine the man lifting us out!

Back home I carefully washed the broken glass out of my hair while my parents went back to the car to collect my things. The SUV was completely destroyed: windshield and windows blown out, body dented, and the hood creased down to a *V* right over the driver's side. Right where I had been seated.

"I can't believe it didn't cave in right on my head!" I said when Mom described it.

"Believe it," she said. She reached into her pocket and pulled out my guardian angel clip. "It was fastened at the exact point where the roof came down," she said. "The angel must have spread his wings to protect you."

Spread his wings—and stretched out his arms to lift me to safety. I was lucky my guardian angel was with us that day. You never know what can happen on the interstate.

Back Draft!

Jeremy Burchfield

What a racket! Were they never going to quiet down? *Some of us are trying to get some sleep!* I thought, pressing my pillow around my head. I'd come to college, tiny Lee University in eastern Tennessee, to get serious about my studies—I couldn't say the same for some of the other guys in my dorm.

I rolled over in my bed on the second floor of Ellis Hall, and stared wide-eyed at the clock on the end table: 2:00 AM. Unbelievable.

In the darkness, I could see my roommate, Aaron, tossing and turning, as well. Outside the door people hollered, some kind of big ruckus. Everyone besides us was apparently having a great time.

I was a freshman music major. It was early November 1993, the school year only a couple months old. So much, still, to get used to. So many things I wasn't sure about. I'd met a girl recently. We'd gone out on a few dates. But was she really that into me? Who could tell? I didn't even know if I was in the right major. I loved music, but not really Bach and Beethoven, the stuff I was studying in my music-theory class. I liked rock and roll, playing electric guitar. Back home in Alabama, friends and I had even started a band.

"God has a plan for your life," my mother always said. "You just need to put your trust in Him. God is always there for you." It wasn't that I didn't believe that, but it was hard to imagine that God was actually looking out for me personally. That He had a specific purpose set out just for me. I was simply hoping to pass music theory. Assuming I ever got to sleep. Now there was some kind of low rumbling noise. *Enough already!*

I switched on the lamp by my bed and stomped to the door. Aaron was right behind me. Someone was going to hear about this.

The doorknob felt warm, almost hot. *Strange.* I flung the door open. There was a whooshing sound. Then a blast of heat. Like I'd been thrown inside a furnace. "Fire!" screamed Aaron. He jerked me back into the room and slammed the door shut.

I couldn't see. The heat had blinded me. I fell to the floor. "We've gotta get out of here!" I heard Aaron yell.

My skin, my hands, my arms, my back. They all felt like they were on fire. The pain was excruciating.

I slowly stood up and took a deep breath, my lungs filling with smoke. I fell back to the floor, choking and coughing. *Dear God, help.* It wasn't a conscious thought. Just a reaction. I knew the fire was coming toward us. I was going to die. I only hoped it would be before the flames reached me.

"Grab hold of my hand!" Aaron said. "We're going to have to go out the window." His voice sounded like it was coming from a million miles away. I could barely make out the words. I felt a hand grab my arm, pulling me, dragging me, across the floor. With every breath I was taking in more smoke, my lungs burning.

"Get a chair," Aaron said. "We need to break the window. It's our only way out." I remembered the air-conditioning unit in the window. He wanted to break the glass above it and . . . then what? We'd have to jump. It seemed crazy. But I knew Aaron was right. This was our only chance. I had to try.

I crawled across the floor, my hands searching for the chair to my desk that I couldn't see. *There! Got it.* I dragged the chair back to where I heard Aaron . . .

Crash! The window shattered. With my last ounce of strength I used the chair to push myself up.

"Let's get out of here," Aaron said. He scrambled out the window but I couldn't do it. My legs collapsed from under me. I lay on the floor, barely conscious, struggling just to draw a shallow breath. I could hear the fire, a rumbling, popping, roaring horror. I knew the door couldn't hold it back much longer. *It's over. There's no one left. No one who can sa—*

I felt the collar of my pajama top slide up my neck, something tugging it. Then my body was lifted off the floor. Something—or someone—was holding me, supporting every inch of my body.

The next thing I knew I was outside, sprawled on top of Aaron in the grass. I looked up and saw flames bursting through the roof, every window, of the dorm.

"I need to help," I said. I tried to stand up. Everything went dark.

I drifted in and out of consciousness after that. When I finally came to I was in an intensive care unit, my hands and arms wrapped in bandages, my mom and dad next to me. They told me I'd suffered second- and third-degree burns.

"The doctor says you're going to be fine," Mom said. "I don't know how you did it. How you managed to jump out of that window."

I thought back to that moment when I was lying helplessly on the floor, five, six feet from the hole in the window unable to move. There was only one explanation for how I'd gotten out. God was watching over me. I imagined Him, for just an instant, stopping whatever else He was doing to send a mighty, all-powerful angel to rescue me. Me, just a mixed-up college kid. I was that important. It was mind-boggling.

I've thought a lot over the last twenty years about the plan God has for my life. There have been plenty of twists and turns. It took nearly a year for me to completely recover from my injuries. That girl I was dating? I ended up marrying her. We have three beautiful children. I teach Web design to high school students.

Something I could have never imagined. The Internet barely existed when I was a freshman studying music at Lee University.

I can't say there's been one amazing accomplishment, something I can point to for why I was saved that night. I don't need to know all God's plans for me. It's enough for me to remember that God and His angels truly are there for all of us. Every day, and every night.

The Angel Came on Wednesday
Ann Cannady

UNTIL THAT INCREDIBLE MORNING, I thought that angels were something you saw on Christmas cards or read about in the Bible. I never conceived of them as beings who could step into our lives.

Seventeen years ago my life was in terrible turmoil. At forty-four, I had recently been diagnosed with uterine cancer. I agonized over the possibility that I might leave my four children motherless. My husband, Gary, a strapping former Air Force master sergeant, was devastated. He had lost his first wife to the same type of cancer. He took me in his arms and with tears streaming down his face said, "I can't bear the thought of losing you."

My doctor scheduled a radical hysterectomy for later in the month at Cape Fear Valley Hospital. Meanwhile, Gary and I did the only thing we could—we prayed. Every day we knelt together and asked God to heal me, to give us time to raise our children. Friends and fellow members of the Haymount United Methodist Church prayed for me, as well. We had everyone we knew praying. But as the surgery date loomed, I felt my faith begin to waver. What lay ahead seemed so frightening. I knew God was a healer, but I didn't know anyone who had ever been healed.

It was the Wednesday before I was to enter the hospital. Gary and I got up and ate breakfast. Again we prayed together.

At about ten o'clock, as Gary was doing some chores around the house and I worked on bills at my desk in the solarium in our front foyer, the doorbell rang. Gary answered it. When he opened the door I heard a deep, melodious voice say, "I've come to tell Ann."

I turned to see a tall black man standing on the doorstep. He was taller than my six-foot-five-inch husband. His skin was ebony and his eyes were a deep, shimmering azure. He looked past Gary and fixed his gaze directly on me. "Ann," he said, "the cancer in your body has been healed."

"How do you know?" I managed to gasp.

"God told me," he answered.

I stared at him uncomprehendingly. I noticed his unusual clothing. He wore a loose, black, gossamer tunic with swirling golden threads, and dark, flowing trousers. His shoes were woven from some ribbonlike material. He was clean-shaven with close-cropped hair, and there was an aura of peace about him.

"Would you like to come in?" I said. I glanced at Gary, who was as awestruck as I. He stepped aside for the man to enter.

"Sir," I said, standing up, "I don't understand. What is your name?"

He smiled radiantly and touched his left shoulder with the index and middle finger of his right hand. "My name is Thomas."

Speaking in the most comforting tones, Thomas told me I must not worry. He quoted Isaiah: "And with his stripes we are healed." And then he said, "Before I go, I must pray for you."

He held out his right palm about twelve inches from my forehead. "Father God," he began, and as he prayed I felt intense heat radiating from his hand. My legs weakened, my eyes closed, and as I fell gently to the floor I was aware of a powerful white light moving up through my body.

I awoke to see Gary leaning over me. "Ann, are you all right?"

"Where is he?" I asked.

But Thomas had vanished.

I crawled to the phone and called my doctor. "Something has happened to me that I can't explain," I said. "I won't need the surgery."

The doctor said he realized how the stress and fear could be affecting my imagination. But I insisted. Finally we compromised. If I would show up for the surgery, he would perform another biopsy as I lay on the operating table before any further procedures were done.

I agreed. And that Sunday I entered the hospital as planned. When I awoke in my room afterward, my doctor was at my bedside shaking his head. "Ann, I can't explain it. Your tissue appears clean. We didn't operate. We'll do further tests, but for now you're in the clear."

In the years since, there has been no recurrence of the cancer. Thomas did not return. But no longer do I think of angels as confined to Christmas cards. I know that they are here among us, doing God's work in our lives.

Stranger on the Ice

Dave Gibbons

I MET MY COUSIN ERIC out on Bald Eagle Lake for what we expected to be an uneventful day of ice fishing. The weather was cloudy and mild for early December, somewhere between mid to upper thirties, and while there were a few other fishermen out on the lake, they were a good two hundred yards away. All signs seemed to point to a peaceful day ahead.

Still, we were careful as we set up our gear. The ice had buckled in on itself while we were out the previous weekend, causing an overflow of water to spill across the surface. The flow started near the shore and worked its way out across the lake. I had to move one of my tip-ups, as it was in the path of the oncoming water.

Throughout the week it looked like everything had frozen solid once again. Windblown snow had crusted over where the water had been, making the precarious places on the ice obvious to anyone who looked. I decided to test the ice myself. Eric and I were both experienced fishermen, but safety was not something either of us took lightly.

I set out across a spot where there had been water the week before. Suddenly, I began to sink as the crusted snow beneath my feet dropped away. I plunged chest-deep into freezing water. I struggled to get back onto the ice, but I could not get my leg on the side of the hole to kick myself out.

"Grab this!" Eric held out an ice pick, getting as close as he dared, but it wasn't close enough. I was able to grasp the pick, but to pull me out Eric would need to come closer. A few more steps and he'd slip into the water with me. I let go of the pick and turned again to see if I could get my foot on the side of the hole. No luck. Icy water saturated my insulated clothes. I couldn't see a way out.

Turning back to Eric I saw a man approaching from behind. "I've got a rope," he said. He tossed the end to me. I grasped it like a lifeline, and the two of them pulled me out of the hole. Relief washed over me.

Out of the corner of my eye I saw the stranger with his rope, walking off in the same direction he had come from. I was too busy counting my blessings to chase after him. Eric and I called it a day, and before we packed up I looked for the man in the distance, but he was gone.

The next day, Eric met me out on the lake again. We chose our fishing spot. There was no way I'd let a small accident scare me away from ice fishing for good, but I knew I was lucky that stranger had shown up. I could see the hole where I'd fallen in the day before. Eric glanced over at it too. "You know," Eric said as we settled in, "I never saw that guy's face."

"I didn't either," I said. Now that I thought about it, the whole rescue seemed impossible. We'd seen how far away the other fishermen were. It would have taken a miracle for one of them to have gotten to us with that rope in time to help me. The stranger seemed to come out of nowhere and to disappear when his job was done. That's why I believe God sent me an angel. A miracle on ice.

The Man in the Three-Piece Suit

Rosemary Marbach

THE BEACH ON LAKE ERIE was a short walk down the street from our house. The four of us: my mom, my sister Lucy, my brother Charlie, and I, headed down the road hoping to go for a swim. The elm tree at the end of the road made way to a dirt path that led us to the wooden stairs that went down to the beach. At the time Lucy was in fourth grade, Charlie in sixth, and I was in third.

It was a gray and windy day. Mom told us if the waves were too high we might not be going in. Lucy and Charlie ran ahead, and I heard Lucy yell, "Last one in is a rotten egg!" My mom yelled back, "Be careful, you two."

As my mom and I made our way down the stairs, we looked out at the water—it looked a bit choppy, but not dangerous. Lucy was already in the water and turned to Charlie with a victorious fist in the air as he stepped in. "I won!" she bellowed. Lucy dove in and leaped back up and had a smile as wide as a Cheshire cat. Charlie strolled into the water, looked out toward Lucy with his hands on his hips and then back to my mother and me as we walked down the wooden stairs to the beach below.

"Lucy won," I said.

A slight smile crossed my mother's lips as she looked down at me. "Don't tease him. It'll just make it worse."

As Mom looked back up to the water, she suddenly let go of my hand and pointed out to Lucy. "Hey, get back here! You're out too far!" she yelled. Her walk quickened, and I tried to keep up as we reached the shore.

"Come on, you two, don't play like that," she continued.

Lucy waved her hands up in the air, bobbed under the waves, and then popped up again. Charlie was up to his waist in the water. He was looking out at Lucy and then turned back to us. "She can't!" he yelled back.

I always thought my mom treated me like a baby when she told me never go in the water alone because the current was really strong. I remember not knowing what a current was, but Charlie said it was like a big vacuum that sucked you far away in the water.

I looked out at Lucy. She had a frozen look on her face as she moved farther away from the shore. Charlie raced out of the water and over to a cement jetty that ran from the shore into the water. He hopped up on the wall and ran down to the end close to where Lucy was and dove right in.

The sand sifted quickly under my toes. I looked up at my mother. Her skin looked as gray as the water and her lipstick was faded. I never sensed fear from my mother but I could now in her voice. "Be careful," she whispered, staring out at Charlie.

I squinted as I looked out to Lucy and Charlie. They were *both* yelling and being taken farther out to sea. My mother looked down at me.

"Step back. Get out of the water. And stay there." She then pointed to the sand and driftwood pile back from the shore. "Don't move." I was still as a statue.

My mother's head turned, scanning the beach in both directions. No one was in sight. She ran to the jetty and shouted something out to Lucy and Charlie, turned, and raced by me toward the shore, screaming, "Somebody, oh, somebody, please help. Oh, God, somebody please help us."

She went to the grassy bank that led to the stairs and repeated her cries. She rushed back, took my hand, and we ran to where the water lapped at our feet. I reached around her legs and hugged them tight. I remember the wind blowing and my mother crying out loudly, "Please, God, please . . ."

I clutched my mother's legs, trying to pray but the words wouldn't come for either of us. Only cries for help. I turned my head and saw a large man in a three-piece brown suit, with pant legs rolled up, striding along the shore toward us. He continued marching right into the water. I remember thinking what big white feet he had. His arms swung as he stomped right by us, eyes straight ahead, and dove into the water. I winced, thinking for sure that my mom was going to break one of my fingers, she was holding my hand so tight. She kept repeating, "Oh, God. Oh, God."

I closed my eyes and the next thing I knew I heard voices—crying and shouting. It was Lucy and Charlie. The man was coming toward us with Lucy and Charlie, each dangling from one of his big arms. Lucy was coughing, her wide blue eyes now red and swollen. Charlie's hair was matted flat across his eyes, his face red, and also coughing and choking. The man stared straight ahead as though my mother and I weren't there.

As the three reached the shore, my mom and I started jumping up and down, and with the break of a wave we were all together, hugging, crying, and spitting out words in incoherent sentences. In our group hug, I saw the man's brown pants. The brown color turned gray, the color of the water. It *was* the water. I turned and looked to the side. No, he wasn't there.

"Mom, where is he? Where'd he go?" I asked.

Still clinging to one another, Lucy, Charlie, and my mother turned, looking in all directions. The long stretch of beach was bare. The walk to the stairway was too far away; he couldn't have made it there without us seeing him. And there were no footprints anywhere.

We were all silent as the water tapped our feet. My mother, still out of breath, repeated over and over, "Thank You, God, thank You, God . . ." We began to slowly walk home, asking those we passed if they saw a man fitting the description of the man in the three-piece suit. No one had seen such a person. We continued walking home in silence, partly in shock or perhaps more in awe.

We all knew what had happened: God sent an angel, a barefoot angel in a three-piece suit to save Lucy and Charlie. Whether in silence or whispers or cries, He always hears our calls. And to this day, whenever I'm near the water and see children playing along the shore, I give thanks.

The Man in the Field

Alice Brawner

"BLACKBERRY COBBLER! I CAN ALREADY TASTE IT," my brother Grady said as we made our way to the field in front of our house. We were on a mission—to fill the new basket swinging on his arm to the brim with ripe, juicy blackberries. He'd admired it in town weeks ago, and so our oldest sister went out and bought it for him. The basket was his to keep, but on one condition:

"You have to fill it with berries," she said. "I'll whip up one of those cobblers you're always going on about." I quickly agreed to help—anything for a piece of that cobbler! We could hardly contain our excitement when we asked our mother if we could go out berry picking.

"Okay," she said. "But don't go any farther than the field in front of the house so I can keep an eye on you."

"We won't!" the two of us declared, and off we went. With the sun at our backs and insects buzzing around our feet we marched across the field. But the blackberry bushes were few and far between, and those we did find had already been picked clean by little sparrows and blackbirds.

"This isn't nearly enough to make a cobbler," Grady sighed, examining the tiny pile of berries at the bottom of the basket.

"What if we try looking in that forest past the viaduct?" I suggested. "I never see anyone there, so I bet there are loads of berries left." Our mother *had* told us to keep to the field by the house, but this was kind of an emergency.

"Guess a quick trip couldn't hurt," Grady said. We set out for the viaduct and, after passing under its sturdy stone archways, found ourselves in another field that led to the forest. "Let's go!" Grady said. He sprinted through the tall grass. I ran after him, visions of cobbler in my head. The forest was much farther away than I'd remembered. I slowed down, panting, after a few minutes of running. *Maybe we should turn back.*

Suddenly, Grady dropped out of sight, his head disappearing beneath the sea of waving, yellow stalks. I hurried to catch up. When I got to him, his legs were buried up to his knees, and he was waving and calling frantically for help. *Quicksand!* Now it wasn't so surprising that we never saw anyone near these woods. They were dangerous!

I reached for Grady. "I'm sinking! I can't get out!" He grabbed my hand. In his panic he nearly pulled me in with him.

I let go and looked desperately around. There wasn't a soul in sight. Should I run for help? Try again to pull him out?

God, I prayed, *what should I do?*

A man appeared, striding through the field. He had a long, flowing white beard and walked at a steady, unhurried speed. I screamed for help, but the man didn't rush his pace. I waved my arms and jumped as high as I could, but the man kept walking.

My brother had sunk into the ground up to his hips by the time the bearded man reached us. He bent down and picked up a branch from the ground. Calm as ever, he held it out for Grady to grab on to. My brother seized the end of the branch and the man hauled him easily back onto safe ground.

I ran over and swept Grady up in a hug, tears of joy running down my face. We cared little anymore about that blackberry cobbler.

The two of us turned to the man to thank him, but he had disappeared. In the distance, across the field, we could see our mother heading for us. The man was nowhere to be seen. I supposed because there hadn't been a man there in the first place. Only an angel. As Grady is my witness.

Miracle Baby

Rose Foster

ROSE WAS THE YOUNGEST of the seven Johnson children, born late in her parents' life, and named after the roses that bloomed in the front yard. This unexpected addition to the family seemed to everyone like a miracle. The entire household took delight in her every coo.

On a May afternoon in 1935, when Rose was ten months old, she'd been down for her nap longer than usual. "I'll go check on her," Mrs. Johnson said to the other children. Her eldest daughter, Bessie, followed her mother into the baby's room, where Mrs. Johnson leaned over the crib and laid a hand on the child's forehead. "This baby is burning up," she said.

"I'll call the doctor," Bessie said. At seventeen, she felt old enough to be the baby's mother herself, and had taken a special interest in her welfare and upbringing from the moment the child was born.

The Johnsons lived on the edge of a small town in the Texas Panhandle, and it took some time before the country doctor arrived. He pressed a stethoscope to Baby Rose's chest, listened, and frowned. "She has pneumonia in both lungs," he said. Bessie looked terrified. Pneumonia? That could be deadly! "There's not much I can do for her, except come back every day and check on her," the doctor said. "Let's hope she starts showing signs of improvement."

But Baby Rose didn't improve. Every day when the country doctor came and listened to her lungs, he would sigh and shake his head. Every night the whole family gathered around the crib and prayed for Baby Rose. The little ones didn't understand the danger, but Bessie was bracing herself for the worst.

Then one morning Bessie went to Rose's crib and found her body contorted. Bessie couldn't wake her. "Mama!" she cried out.

Mrs. Johnson had fallen asleep in a chair by the crib. She jumped up to see. "Oh, Lord," she said. "Go get the doctor. Quick!"

The doctor came, but there was little he could do. "She has spinal meningitis," he said. By then Rose's breathing was labored. "She's in a coma. She may not recover, and if she does she'll spend her life in a wheelchair."

"God, let Rose get well, even if she'll need a wheelchair," Bessie said.

"We'll take care of her no matter what," one little brother promised.

"Just don't take her away from us!" another brother said.

Every passing day the doctor kept up his visits and neighbors brought food and poultices. The family prayed little Rose would survive. Bessie perhaps prayed hardest of all. She didn't stop praying either, the day the doctor told the family that Baby Rose was dying. "She'll probably pass sometime this evening," he said.

That night the Johnson family ate dinner in silence. As she was helping with the dishes Bessie looked out the kitchen window. "Storm's coming, Mama," she said. In the Texas Panhandle that was no small announcement. Within thirty minutes wind beat the shutters against the house, and long fingers of lightning ignited the sky. First it rained, and then it hailed, golf-ball–sized pieces of ice falling from heaven. Normally a storm of this magnitude would have the whole house in an uproar—the younger kids crying, the parents wondering if it was time to head to the tornado cellar in the backyard. But everyone's heart was so heavy about Rose that nothing else seemed to matter. The family sat in the living room and Rose's mother kept watch by the crib. They barely noticed the chunks of ice battering the roof, or the wind howling at the door.

In typical Texas fashion, the storm passed as quickly as it had arrived. The rain and hail stopped abruptly, and in minutes the sky was clear and calm. That's when Bessie heard her mother running through the house. "Our baby is well!" Mrs. Johnson shouted out. "Our baby is well!" Everyone ran into Rose's room and peered into the crib. She lay straight on her back, eyes wide open.

When the country doctor arrived the next morning he had no explanation for Rose's rapid turnaround. "That's not entirely true," he said. "There is one explanation, and He sits on His throne in heaven."

Bessie thought back to the storm. It had arrived out of nowhere just when Baby Rose was about to slip away. It was as if every drop of rain, every piece of hail, every gust of wind had carried angels descending onto a small patch of the Texas Panhandle to witness the miracle healing of a baby whose very birth had been a miracle. God's second miracle for a family who loved their Baby Rose above all else.

Rose went on to lead a long, healthy life, never suffering any symptoms from her pneumonia and spinal meningitis. Never needing a wheelchair as the doctor had predicted. Never tiring of hearing the story of her healing from her sister Bessie, especially, who never tired of telling it at every Johnson family gathering. And though it was long, long ago that angels came for a baby during a ferocious storm, I know this story to be true. You see, I am Rose. I am that miracle baby.

Angels Are Watching over Me
Alice M. McGhee

EVERYTHING WENT BLACK, but it wasn't "black." All I could see were swirls of pink and blue.

The colors moved as if someone were making cotton candy with pink- and blue-colored sugar spinning in the machine. I heard only silence—but it was deafening. I felt as if I were going to die.

"If you are ready for me, I am ready for you," I told Jesus in my heart.

Everything stopped. As I sat in my car, I knew the engine had stalled, but it felt like my body was still spinning. The top of my head hurt horribly. As my jumbled mind tried to figure out where I was, I tried to open the driver's side door of the car, but it would not open.

The car had landed in the midst of a grove of saplings. The driver's side door was pushed against them so tightly it could not open. I became vaguely aware of cars and trucks moving along on the highway above me, way above me. I wasn't sure where I was. I wondered if I had died and gone to heaven.

There was a knock on the front passenger-side door. An average-looking man with sandy hair and glasses, who was wearing a red shirt, said, "Lady, are you all right?"

He was not wearing a coat even though it was snowing hard and the ground was icy. I was not sure where he had come from or how he had gotten there.

"I think I'm okay, but I'm not sure."

"We need to get you out of this car. It's leaking gas. Can you crawl to the passenger-side door in the backseat?"

"I think I can."

"Move back that way and I'll try to help you. No, wait! Your car is at a precarious angle. Come out the front passenger door. I'm afraid the car might tip over if you try to get out by any other way. Move very carefully!"

As I slid across the seat toward the sound of his voice, I was not afraid. I trusted him completely, even though we had never met.

Mr. Red Shirt said, "Let's move away from the car. You have a gas leak. The odor is pretty strong."

I gradually became more aware of my surroundings. I did smell the pungent odor from the leaking gas. There was a steep slope a short distance away from my car, and I realized that the hill was covered with snow and ice.

The snow had been falling for quite a while. I wondered how I would be able to climb up to the road. I walked toward the slope that led to the road, but it was difficult due to the slick and uneven ground.

My new friend told me to take his arm and he would help me climb the hill. As I placed my arm through his, the grass was no longer slippery. Walking up the hill became easy, even though the ground was still covered with ice and snow.

I heard a siren and saw the flashing lights of a fire truck. As my friend and I reached the interstate highway at the top of the hill, I was placed into the caring hands of the firefighters.

One of the firefighters asked where my car was.

"It's down at the bottom by some trees."

He went down into the ravine to be sure no one else had been in the car with me. It took him quite a while to find the car because the snow and darkness hindered his visibility.

The firefighter who had been searching for my car returned to the ambulance and said, "Most people who park their cars that far from the highway don't walk away from them! No one else is in your car. I think you should keep driving big, heavy cars like that Park Avenue. The size of that car is probably one reason you're alive."

"Where is the man in the red shirt who got me out of the car and helped me up the hill? I want to thank him for his help."

"He was standing right here next to the ambulance just a minute ago," one of the men said. "Hey, John, have you seen the guy wearing the red shirt who saw the accident? I was looking for him so I could ask him a few questions. It was like he just disappeared. He was here and then he wasn't. I didn't even see his car. I have no idea how he got out here. It is the weirdest thing I have ever seen."

The ambulance ride to the hospital was uneventful. After a CAT scan, the doctors decided I was in remarkably good condition and could go home.

With my head still pounding, my husband and I drove to the repair shop where my car had been towed. At first it didn't look too bad, but the mechanic told us the frame of the car had been twisted, the motor had been knocked off the mounting, and the gas tank was ruptured.

The strangest thing was that each of the foot compartments had been shoved upward nearly to the bottom of the seats, except for one—the one in front of the driver's seat.

"I like your bumper sticker," the mechanic said, "the one that says 'Angels are watching over me.' I know somebody was watching over you, or you would not have walked away from that banged-up car the way you did."

I learned to trust God with *everything* on that night. Trusting myself was not enough. Not only did God watch over me when I had not asked Him to, but He had a whole army of angels there—including one wearing a red shirt!

A Mother's Hope

Tiffini Dingman-Grover

SOMETHING WAS WRONG WITH MY SON DAVID. He was a big kid, eight years old, 150 pounds, but he had lost his appetite. He'd stopped telling jokes, too, stopped being his usual happy-go-lucky self. His jaw hurt for no discernible reason. He began throwing up. We thought David was suffering side effects from his medication for attention-deficit disorder. Then he threw up in the car on the way to his favorite restaurant, and the pediatrician told us to get him to a hospital immediately. The emergency-room doctor was young, a resident. He checked David over, shined a light down his throat. He was so shocked by what he saw, he uttered something I can't repeat in polite company. The doctor apologized and said, "We need an MRI immediately." I noticed the nurse crying. What did she know that I didn't? Hours later, at 2:00 AM, I found out. The diagnosis was still imprecise, but David was being admitted— to the oncology ward. "A massive growth is pushing into your son's throat," the doctor said.

"Mommy, what's wrong with me?" David asked.

"You're going to be okay, sweetheart."

"You'll make it go away, right, Mommy?"

"Of course I will."

They gave David pain medication and he soon fell asleep. My husband, Bryn, and I lay on the floor. The room had a recliner chair, but neither of us could figure out how to work it. My mother-in-law had already taken our two older boys, Matthew and Keith, home. In the dark I tried to pray. But all that came at first were memories.

David was our youngest child, our baby. I loved him more than I knew it was possible to love anyone. We had a good-night ritual we went through no matter what kind of day it had been. I would say, "You." He would say, "Me." And together we would say, "Forever. Sleep with the angels, roses on the pillow, sleep with Jesus."

You, me, forever. Lying on that cold hospital floor, I felt fear and anger build. Twice before David I had gotten pregnant only to lose the baby. *God, You didn't give me David just to take him away, did You?* A piece of medical equipment beeped. *Can You at least give me some kind of answer? Some reassurance?* Silence. I waited in that silence a long time. No answer came. *Fine,* I finally decided. *I'll do it myself.* David was going to live. No power on earth would take my boy from me.

David did have cancer, in one of the worst places possible, at the base of his skull. His particular cancer was called rhabdomyosarcoma, an aggressive tumor spreading across much of the left side of his face and pressing on his carotid artery and optical nerve. It was why his jaw had hurt and he had felt so sick. It also explained his mood swings. The tumor was right next to his brain. So close, in fact, that surgery was out of the question. David's only chance was intensive chemotherapy and radiation. Even then, only half of kids diagnosed with his kind of cancer survived five years.

Those odds didn't daunt me. I was determined to will David back to health. Bryn and I both worked for a computer software company—I handled finances, Bryn managed the warehouse—and our bosses generously allowed us to take time off and work odd shifts to spend as many days and nights with David as possible. We became his nurses, his coaches, his constant companions. He had an

IV line inserted in his chest. We learned how to clean it and check for infection. His eyes developed nystagmus from the pressure on the optical nerve. We made certain his patch stayed in place. When he had trouble breathing, we held the oxygen mask to his mouth.

As David's treatment advanced, doctors told Bryn and me that his chances were even worse than most kids'. The cancer was too deeply entrenched. I refused to be discouraged. Although the chemotherapy left David skinny and weak, I urged him out of bed every day to walk down the hall.

We reached our insurance company's one-million-dollar coverage cap in eleven months. After that, we faced bills up to fourteen hundred dollars a week. *Not going to stop us,* I thought. I began selling off clothes and other things around the house. Much later, when we learned that only an expensive experimental surgery had a chance of saving David, I even went on eBay and put up for auction one of the "Frank Must Die" bumper stickers Bryn had made—"Frank" was our family nickname for David's cancer, short for Frankenstein. I told potential bidders I was trying to raise money for my son's cancer care. Amazingly, we got some media coverage—a reporter at our small hometown paper happened to know someone at the *Washington Post*—and money came in. The support was wonderful. Still, David wasn't getting any better.

One night in the hospital he sat up in bed and said, "Mom, the angels came to talk to me. It's time for me to go."

I peered at him through the dimness, fighting to stay calm. Was he dreaming? "You saw angels, David?"

"They're here with me now, Mom. It's time to go. I'm tired."

I struggled to control my voice. "Sweetheart, I know you're tired. But you're not ready to go. Fight. Stay with me. Just stay with me a little while longer."

I rushed out of the room and told the nurses, then called Bryn and asked him to gather everyone. I was about to start praying when a nurse came up to me. "Tiffini, I'm sorry. David's vital signs are very low. This could be the end. We've done everything we can for him. His little body is worn out."

I went back to David's room and sat in a chair in the dark. Again, my fear surged and I felt it form into words. I started to pray, then stopped. Something pressed on me, some resistance. God? Or just my own exhaustion? I was deeply tired. Tired of fighting. Tired of fruitless hope. *Why, God? Why? He's mine. You can't take him!* Again the pressure, the resistance. Only this time it had a shape, almost like a blanket settling over me. A calmness, a sense of release. I heard words: *David is a gift. Love him. Don't own him.* The calmness deepened and I found myself repeating that word, "gift." I had been trying so hard, throwing every ounce of strength into David's life. What if that life wasn't mine to have, to direct according to my will? What if the best thing I could do for David was give him to God? *Lord, David's life is a gift from You, not me. Let Your will be done.*

I looked up. Our entire family was there. They kissed David and said good-bye. When they left, Bryn and I sat together in the room, holding each other, crying and praying. We didn't stop until 7:00 AM, when David suddenly sat up. We looked at the monitors. His vital signs were normal.

"What are you guys doing?" he asked.

"David? Are you all right?" I asked.

"Um, yeah."

"Can you remember anything at all about last night?"

David cocked his head. "You mean about Jesus? Sure. He told me I could stay awhile longer. There's more for me to do."

"You . . . talked to Jesus? Did you actually see Him?"

David made a face. "Mom, come on. He was too bright. I could only see the angels. They were gold."

"But you feel okay?" I asked.

"Yes, I feel fine."

Today David is a challenging thirteen-year-old. The road has not been easy. Radiation and chemotherapy did not rid him of cancer. We ended up taking him to Los Angeles for an experimental surgery that removed nearly all of his tumor.

Sometimes I think of the anger I felt that awful first night in the emergency room, my fist-shaking on the cold hospital floor. I don't blame myself for it. I'm a mother, after all. And I suppose I needed to pass through that anger to learn the lesson of my son's illness. As is common with kids who survive cancer, David lives with side effects from radiation and surgery. He has good days and bad days. Yet he and I both know that each and every day is a gift. And that it is a blessing to say each night, "You, me, forever."

Angel on a Raft

Roseli Fonfrias

AFTER SPENDING THE MORNING TOURING Rio de Janeiro's Corcovado Mountain where the statue of the Christ stood, my friends and I were ready to take on Ipanema Beach.

The sand was very hot as we walked in search of a good spot to lay down our blanket. Even though the surf was particularly rough, I decided to walk over to the edge of the water to cool off my feet.

Ignoring my friend's warnings about this particular section being dangerous because of its undertow, I assured them I was only dipping my toes. Next thing I knew, I felt a current so powerful that it dropped me to my knees. *I must look silly here in one foot of water, unable to stand up on my own two feet*, I thought. When I looked back at the girls I noticed they were pointing at a sign that said **Perigo** (meaning "danger" in Portuguese) that stood prominently in the sand.

This was the very sign we were instructed by our travel coordinator to look out for. But it was too late. The next thing I remember happening was being underneath a powerful wave that pulled me underwater and twisted me around like a cyclone. I couldn't tell if I was up or down—and my arms and legs were being pulled in every direction. When I finally managed to come up for air, only my arms were free but my feet felt like they were inside of a flushing apparatus.

Nothing prepared me for coming up to the surface of the water, and seeing that the distance between myself and the shoreline had widened significantly. The people on the shoreline looked so small.

Fighting to stay above water against such a strong undertow was like nothing I had ever experienced. There was absolutely no one else in this section of the ocean. I didn't see any lifeguards and no one was coming in after me. Thoughts of drowning became inevitable when I couldn't keep my legs from tangling up as I treaded the strong currents relentlessly pulling me under. A tremendous sadness settled on me as I thought of my family. I looked up and saw the statue of Christ on Corcovado Mountain with His arms stretched out and felt a quiet peace come over me as I prayed for His help.

I couldn't believe what I saw next. Out of nowhere, a boy of about twelve years of age was swimming toward me on top of a two-by-two-foot white Styrofoam float. He was bobbing up and down on the choppy water yelling at me in Portuguese. I reached out to him but my legs were paralyzed. The strong currents kept pushing both of us in every direction except closer to one another. With all my strength, I stretched out my arms and touched the float. He was still yelling as if he wanted me to hold on, but the float kept slipping away from me. I just couldn't get a good grip on it; each time I reached out the current pulled me under. Then, when I came up I noticed that he had gotten off the float and began pushing it toward me. Even under these dire circumstances, I had enough sense to know that if he got off and I got on, I would never be able to live with myself if he drowned.

Right there in the middle of all of this chaos, he nodded his head reassuring me to climb on it. I climbed onto the float and both of us together, him holding on with one hand, paddled our way back. All I remember was screaming in English, "Please don't let go, please don't let go." As I frantically paddled, I could feel him on my right pushing us forward even though the swells of the waves kept pushing our little life raft back. He kept my spirits up as he yelled above the loud sounds of the ocean in Portuguese as we got closer and closer to the beach. When I felt my feet drag the sand below me, I watched as my friends rushed over and pulled me back to safety.

When I felt my feet touch the sand beneath me, I turned around and placed my hand on his head. We were still in the water. There was so much chaos with my girlfriends rushing toward me and everyone talking at the same time. No one could hear me through my coughs as I pleaded, "Where's the boy, where's the boy?"

One girl who worked with me as a legal secretary in New York said, "He's gone, he just ran off."

Sitting there catching my breath, I continued looking to my right and to my left hoping he would return. I'm not going to say it doesn't break me up whenever I think about what happened. I still can't believe it. This boy didn't wait for a reward or a simple thank-you. The only time I actually had a good look at his face was when we were out in the middle of the ocean.

I never saw the boy again, but think about him almost every day. Also, whenever I look at the beautiful wooden souvenir I brought home with me of the Christ statue, I give thanks. I like to think that the Christ that stood on the mountain and watched me pleading for my life actually extended His arms and placed this beautiful angel on a raft to save me.

Giant Warrior Angels

Rennie Duncan

I SHOULD HAVE FOLLOWED THE RULES. As a very white-skinned, blue-eyed, blonde missionary in Uganda, Africa, I was not supposed to leave the area unless I was escorted by Ugandan men. I was told that if I went out unescorted, the possibility was great that I might be harmed.

But what was I to do? I had promised to speak at a bush church that Sunday but no Ugandan men were available to escort me. I had no way to communicate to the pastor of that church that I wouldn't be there. I loved the Ugandan people and that pastor and the last thing I wanted to do was break my promise.

A missionary nurse friend knew how much I wanted to honor my commitment. She owned an SUV, assured me that she knew the way to that church, about an hour and a half from the orphanage I had come there to start, and she offered to drive me there. After much thought (and not enough prayer), I grabbed my cell phone and decided to take the chance without male escorts.

The dirt roads had no street or road signs and were often no more than goat paths. We traveled the path until it disappeared and then drove across a field scattered with brush. When the field of matoki trees (a type of banana) became too rugged to continue driving, we stopped and walked the last half mile to the church. It was hot and humid. The flies buzzed around our faces and the long grasses scraped at our legs beneath our ankle-length skirts. When we reached the church that was built with straw and held together with cow and goat dung, we were hot, tired, and sweaty. The congregation was seated and waiting for me.

After the service, we walked back to the vehicle and drove along the goat trail, then onto a dirt road. After a few miles steam began to rise from under the hood and the vehicle stopped. The temperature gauge was in the red. At one glance around me I knew we were in deep trouble. Our vehicle was stalled across the street from a banana beer bar where Ugandan men hang out.

My friend called her mechanic with my cell phone and was attempting to give him our location when several Ugandan men walked out of the bar. One of them pointed toward us and they all looked our way. Then they began sauntering toward us, laughing and hitting each other's arms as they gestured in our direction. I prayed, "God, You know the trouble we're in. These men know we're two vulnerable Muzungu [white] women with no men to protect us. Please surround our vehicle with angels. And, God, please make them giant, warrior angels even bigger than the seven-foot Karamajong warriors who guard our orphanage— warriors who will stop these men from reaching us."

I kept praying out loud for giant warrior angels, yet I could hear my heart beating above my own words. My hands shook as I rolled up the windows and locked the doors. Being about fifty miles from the equator, it was only seconds before we were wet with perspiration. I remembered that we didn't have much water left. My fear and the suffocating air inside the SUV were making me feel nauseated as I watched the laughing men swagger toward us.

When the men were about fifty feet from our vehicle they all stopped suddenly and took a few steps backward. They stared in our direction with fear on their faces, mumbled something to each other, then turned and rushed back into the bar.

I quickly rolled down the windows and took a few deep breaths before I gave thanks to our mighty God for surrounding us with warrior angels fierce enough to frighten those men. I wish I could have seen the angels too. But it didn't matter. I knew they were there; and I could visualize them, dressed in black pants, T-shirts, and stocking caps, carrying bows and arrows; like the biggest and most feared warriors in Africa; who intimidated those men by their mere presence.

I had learned my lesson. I realized that the rules were created for our safety, and that was the first and last time I failed to follow the rules.

It Sparked!

Elizabeth A. Nixon

WHEN MY SON, JOSHUA, was three years old, he was playing in my bedroom while I was getting ready to go out one morning. He had taken some of my hair bands and hair clips to play with on the floor.

I was in the adjoining master bathroom doing my hair when I smelled an acrid odor, the smell of wire burning, and heard a sizzling *zzzzzp* sound.

I ran into the bedroom and saw Joshua sitting on the floor with a very shocked look on his face. He was holding his fingers and had huge saucer eyes, although he wasn't crying. When he looked up at me, it was with one of those "Am I going to get into trouble?" looks.

I looked at the wall and saw a black mark coming out of the electrical outlet and streaking up the wall above it. The outlet itself was covered in black and a melted plastic and metal clip was in the outlet.

It was one of those awful moments as a mom when you have that sinking feeling in your stomach. In an instant you're rethinking the whole situation and already putting the blame squarely on yourself.

Running over to him, I asked, "Are you okay?"

He nodded his head but held up his fingers. I held them and kissed them, and he began to cry, more from being frightened than because his fingers hurt.

"What happened?" I asked. "Did you put one of Mummy's clips in the outlet?"

In his little quiet voice he said, "Mummy, it sparked!"

I could see the result of that spark halfway up the wall. The black mark was an awful sight. I was in shock, too, and really surprised that Joshua hadn't been hurt more, given the burned area on the wall and the melted clip hanging out of the outlet. In fact, I couldn't believe he had no marks on his fingers or hand and that he hadn't been shocked.

I asked him what happened.

He said, "I put your clip in there and it sparked, a big spark, and my angels did this."

Then he threw himself on the bed, two feet away, and started shaking his entire body.

"What?" I said.

He said, "When the spark came out, my angels did this." And again he threw himself backward across the bed and began shaking his body.

"The angels took the shock for you?" I asked. I was trying to understand what he was telling me.

He smiled a big, laughing smile, as if it was a funny joke, and started shaking himself all over the bed. He was clearly already over any fright he'd had.

Now it was clear what he was telling me. The reason he had not been hurt from the electrical shock—which had burned up the clip and the outlet and left a blackened, burned mark halfway up the wall—was that his angels had taken the electrical shock for him! In doing so, Joshua's angels literally were thrown two feet across the room and onto the bed, where they shook and shook from the electrical force.

I have heard of angels being physically wounded when fighting a spiritual battle for us, and I still don't understand the dynamics of how that happens. How is it that these angelic beings, who are spirit in nature, enter our natural realm and experience earthly things in their bodies?

I have to say, I don't really know how it works, but I am really glad it does. Because that morning Joshua's angels may just have saved his life!

"I Can't Move, I Can't Breathe!"
Gloria Farah

TODAY THE RIVERBANK WHERE OUR LITTLE BOYS, **Douglas** and Dennis, nearly lost their lives is covered with vines. But on that awful day in May, the growth had been cut back because a new drainpipe was to be installed.

The whole family loved our jungle headquarters—loved it mostly because of the friends we'd made there. With a dozen other Wycliffe families we'd started the work in this remote area. Together we'd faced crushing handicaps, struggling against indifference and hostility as we tried to translate the Bible into local tribal languages, and against mosquitoes, parasites, and poisonous snakes as we tried to carve a home out of the jungle.

Because of our translation work we were immersed day and night in the Bible. And over the months, a strange thing took place. The Bible began to happen. Instead of being a sacred collection of ancient stories, the Bible became an experience. We discovered that we could pray for the sick and have them get well. We experienced the fact of Christ's power over evil. And in our own family we came to know for ourselves just how real a creature a child's guardian is. Jesus tells us that a child's angel is in heaven, always looking into the face of the Father (see Matthew 18:10). How important, for us, this fact became.

Our son Doug was seven years old, his big brother Dennis nine that spring. I remember how, on the night before the accident, my husband, David, was putting the boys down when Doug propped himself up on his elbow.

"Daddy, can we build a cave with our knives?"

David saw no reason to say no: how could two little boys build much of a cave with pocket knives? "Sure you can, Doug."

It wasn't, of course, until weeks later that we pieced together all that happened that next day. Doug and his older brother were playing pirates with several other mission children. They dug their cave in the cleared earth, then most of the pirates left to go swimming, leaving only Doug and Dennis and a friend named Mark at the cave entrance.

Doug saw his brother stick his head and shoulders into the shallow cave—with all their work, their tunnel went only a few feet into the dry mud bank. Doug heard Dennis's voice calling from inside the cave. "Come on in."

Doug began to crawl in. A bed of red ants had been disturbed, but the boys ignored them.

Then, with no warning, the dry mud shifted. In one instant the steep bank slid silently down on our two boys and trapped them beneath its suffocating mass.

Mark was covered, too, but wiggled free and started to shout and to dig with his hands. "Dennis! Doug! Where are you!"

There was no answer, no movement. Mark began to cry for help.

Inside the cave, Doug had been slapped down on his chest. His face was smashed into the dirt, but a pocket of air helped him breathe.

"Dennis, can you hear me?"

His voice seemed to make no sound at all, but he felt a slight movement beneath him. "Dennis," Doug went on. "I can't move. I can't breathe!"

He felt another wiggle. An ant crawled onto his face, then another. The first sting came. It was on his eyelid.

"Dennis, I can't talk . . . the air's going away."

The ants were all over him now, stinging. "Dennis, I think we're maybe going to die." He began to struggle. Dirt filled his mouth.

And then Doug stopped talking. He even stopped struggling for air. For there, next to him, was an angel. He stood bright, strong.

"Dennis!" Doug called softly, his voice relaxed. "Dennis, there's an angel here. I can see him plain as anything. He's bright. He's trying to help us." Doug felt one oh-so-slight movement.

"He's not doing anything. But Dennis . . . if we die now . . . it's not so bad . . ." Doug lost consciousness.

Up above, Mark arrived at our house screaming that Dennis and Doug had been buried. David was out in the jungle, but I ran to the cave-in. Men followed me with picks and shovels.

The slide was smooth, like a child's sand castle collapsed. The men began to probe the red earth with sticks.

"Quick, Mark," I begged, "show the men where to dig."

Mark hurled himself down the bank. He stopped, looking around. Then, "Here!" He pointed to a spot on the earth fall. The men jumped forward. Seconds later one of the shovels touched softness. Seconds again and Doug's back and legs were free. Strong arms pulled him from the earth. Dennis's form appeared beneath him.

Neither boy was breathing. Their skin was blue. They lay on the red earth, their bodies so terribly small. Someone began to pray. Someone else ran for oxygen from the airbase.

Then Doug moved. A moment later Dennis stirred. The oxygen arrived. We gave it to Dennis first, then to Doug.

"Mommy!" Doug said as soon as he opened his eyes. "Do you know what I saw? An angel."

"*Shh*, sweetheart. Don't try to talk yet."

By noon next day the doctor allowed the boys to get up. Another two minutes, he told us, and the lack of oxygen would have damaged the boys' brains. But because they had not spent themselves struggling, the doctor said, they had just exactly enough oxygen to come through the experience without damage. And the reason they had not struggled, all of us knew, was the angel—the angel who kept them from being afraid.

Doug lorded it over his friends all that day and for several days following. "I've got a real, live angel," Doug said, until finally even his friend Mark had had enough.

"Oh, quit bragging, Doug. Everybody's got a guardian angel!"

And, of course, the marvel is that Mark is right.

With a Cast on His Leg

Debbie Lewis

FEBRUARY 17, MY BIRTHDAY. As the bus slowed, approaching my stop, I wondered how we'd celebrate. Maybe Jim would take me out to dinner.

Brrr. I shivered as I stepped off the overheated bus into the wintry night. The cold air bit into my face and I turned up my coat and wound the warm scarf tightly around it. So dark! For at least the hundredth time I wished for a streetlight here in this dark neighborhood.

Stepping off the curb my foot hit a patch of gravel and I slipped, wrenching my ankle. In my effort to keep from falling, I spun around and fell—hard—onto the injured foot.

Pain shot up my leg in waves. I screamed, but there was no one to hear—the bus had gone. "Oh, God, dear God," I cried, "I can't stand it!"

I didn't know until later that the jagged edge of a broken bone had actually pierced the flesh near my ankle. All I knew was that I couldn't get up off the sidewalk, and the slightest movement caused such terrible pain that I was afraid I'd pass out.

Why did I call for God? I wondered later, because at the time I didn't believe God existed. Although my family had always gone to church, it somehow had never touched me. Not in any real way. In college I'd decided it wasn't reasonable or rational to believe in someone you couldn't see or hear.

I shouted again. "Help! Someone please help!" Silence. Light shone from the nearby houses behind closed blinds, but no one moved, no one came. "Someone, please help me," I sobbed, shivering against the icy concrete. The only sound was the wind whistling down the narrow street.

Then I heard halting footsteps, and a man appeared from around the corner, with a walking cast on one leg. Awkwardly, he knelt beside me. "It's going to be all right—there's nothing to be afraid of." He reached out and touched my leg. Amazingly, the pain stopped. Again he said, "You'll be all right—you're going to be all right. See, I broke my foot, too, and it's just fine." Then he left, but suddenly there were other people around me, including a nurse and a paramedic.

The nurse called 911, and the next thing I knew, EMTs were lifting me into an ambulance and we were speeding toward the hospital. The technician worked to get me into a more comfortable position, and then she said, "You have a compound fracture. Do you know what that is?" I shook my head, and she told me that the broken bones had separated, and one of the sharp ends was protruding through the skin, just above the ankle. "You must be in terrible pain."

"No," I replied, "I can't feel anything—not since that man touched me." I remained pain free until they sedated me for surgery. When I awoke, I had pins and a plate in my ankle. The surgeon said, using the same words as the man with the cast, "You're going to be all right—you'll be just fine!"

I was, indeed. More than all right. I went from believing there was no God to becoming a woman of faith, because I knew that through His mysterious messenger—surely an angel—God Himself had heard my cries and touched me. It was the best birthday present ever.

Watch thou, dear Lord, with those who wake,

or watch, or weep tonight, and give thine angels

charge over those who sleep.

—SAINT AUGUSTINE

CHAPTER 2

Safe in Their Care

Then he lay down under the bush and fell asleep.

All at once an angel touched him and said, "Get up and eat."

He looked around, and there by his head was some bread

baked over hot coals, and a jar of water. He ate and

drank and then lay down again.

—1 KINGS 19:5–6 (NIV)

Life Lesson

Jennie Bailor

SUMMER WAS SUPPOSED TO BE free of worries for a high school grad like me. No studying, no homework—at least not till I went away to college in the fall. I even had a good secretarial job at an industrial company so I could go off with some money in my pocket.

But one afternoon, while I tried to concentrate on entering orders into my computer, doubts crowded in: I'd never been on my own before. I was shy. I'd always lived in the same small town. How would I make it out there in the big, scary world? I knew Mom would remind me that my guardian angel would be by my side, but I was getting a little too old for that kind of reassurance.

"See you tomorrow," I said to my supervisor before clocking out. I pushed open the warehouse door and headed outside to the parking lot. Mom's little silver Toyota shone in the blazing sun. Mom had saved a long time to buy it, her pride and joy. I got behind the wheel and headed home.

Then everything went black.

I opened my eyes in a strange room. Mom was there. I tried to sit up, but I couldn't move. I was freezing cold. My whole body was sore. My head felt like iron—too heavy to lift.

"What happened?" I mumbled.

"You were in an accident," Mom said. "Everyone's okay. Rest." I fell back to sleep, barely understanding her words.

Hours later a nurse helped me to shuffle into the bathroom for the first time. I stared into the mirror. Thirty-some stitches held my face together; smaller cuts marred the spaces in between. *My guardian angel sure wasn't by my side in the accident,* I thought. Still, compared to what I'd done, my face was nothing. Mom and the police officers had finally told me the truth: The accident was all my fault. I'd made the worst mistake of my life. Witnesses had seen me make a left turn on Route 37—right into the path of a white van going sixty miles per hour. My Toyota—Mom's almost-new silver Camry—spun out into someone's front yard. I was knocked unconscious. Miraculously, the driver of the van wasn't hurt. No one was, except me.

About a week after I was released from the hospital, a police officer came to the house, citing me for the accident and assigning me a court date. "You're lucky you didn't have a passenger in that car," he said.

"We have a lot to be thankful for," Mom said. She put her arm around my shoulder. I still had no memory of the crash. I just knew that I could never make up for my mistake. I could see it on the policeman's face. I'd frightened a lot of people, caused a lot of damage. *God must be so disappointed in me.*

Mom and I went to see her car before it was junked. The passenger door was completely smashed in. "It's just a car," Mom said. "What's important is that you're okay. Everyone's okay." That policeman was right about how lucky I was not to have had a passenger.

"What's this?" I said, reaching through the broken window. On the seat was a bandanna. Like everything else in the car, it was covered in blood.

"That must belong to the man who helped you," said Mom. "Remember, I told you about him."

One of the witnesses at the scene was a man on a motorcycle. He'd stayed with me, trying to clean my face with his bandanna, until paramedics arrived.

"We should wash this and return it to him," said Mom. I knew she was looking for something, anything, I could do to feel better about myself. Maybe this would help.

Finding the man turned out to be easy enough. He worked at a barber shop not far from the site of the accident. Mom and I dropped in and waited until he was between clients.

"I hope you're feeling better," he said when I handed him the bandanna. Coming face-to-face with someone who'd been so kind to me only reinforced my guilt. I held back tears.

"Thank you for everything," I managed, and turned with Mom to go.

"Hey," the man said, "by the way…" We looked back at him. "How's your passenger?"

Mom and I glanced at each other. "Jennie was by herself that day," she reminded him.

"That's what I told the policeman," the barber said. "After the ambulance took Jennie away, he asked me some questions. I told him Jennie was alone. The cop looked confused. According to the driver of the van, there was a second person in the Toyota. Saw them both, he said, right before impact. The van driver was so sure, the cop and I started to think we must've made a mistake."

For the rest of that summer I thought a lot about what the barber said. How the policeman must still have been trying to make sense of what had happened when he mentioned that I'd been lucky I had no passenger. I still had a lot of challenges. The judge had me attend a community class on road safety and write an essay about how I could improve my driving. Both helped me look to the future instead of beating myself up over the past. My confidence behind the wheel returned.

By the time I left for college I was ready for the big world out there, and whatever it held. I knew I'd be okay, because I wasn't exactly on my own. My "passenger" would always be by my side, no matter what, just like Mom always said.

Miracle on the Base
Thomas Waller

THE PHONE RANG JUST AS I was climbing into bed. My wife rolled her eyes. I knew what she was thinking. In my job, a ten o'clock call meant only one thing: an issue over at the Air Force Base. A problem that needed my attention, my expertise. A problem people were counting on me to get fixed. Pronto.

I grabbed the receiver. One of my coworkers wasn't feeling well. He begged me to relieve him. "I'll be right over," I said. At least it wasn't something worse. "Anything I should know?"

"Boiler's acting up. I can't get it to stay on. The building's getting cold, so bring a sweater."

Boiler trouble? It was winter, freezing cold, even here in Northern Mississippi. And tonight, of all nights, the temperature inside the Flight Simulator Building I maintained had to be kept at a constant seventy-six degrees with 60 percent humidity.

I got dressed and kissed my wife good-bye, making a mental note of all the things I'd have to do. My staff and I constantly monitored the heating and air-conditioning, the humidity, the electricity, everything to ensure that this building, with its sixteen state-of-the-art simulators and highly sensitive computers and electronic equipment, could operate 24–7 without even a hiccup. A drop of even a few degrees could be catastrophic. The Air Force brass was coming in the morning for a full-scale dog and pony show, a complete run-through for all the new flight simulators. A super-big deal. The kind of day that could make or break a career.

Still, I wasn't *that* worried as I drove over. I was thirty-four, a veteran aerospace engineer, a rocket scientist. Out of college I'd worked as part of the support team for the Apollo space program and helped put a man on the moon. A boiler was basically a giant hot-water heater. Nothing to it. The important thing was to see that it was back online ASAP.

I got to the Flight Simulator Building in twenty minutes and went straight to the boiler. It was huge—eight feet tall, six feet wide—with a series of switches and handles to control it. The tank connected to a maze of pipes that delivered hot water, exactly 180 degrees, throughout the building's heating system.

"Okay," I said, "let's get you up and running." The building was quiet, not another soul around. I turned a knob a bit to the right, then the next one to the left. There was a set sequence that had to be followed precisely to reset the boiler. I listened for it to fire up. *Good.* There was nothing to do but wait. It took about thirty minutes for the boiler to run through the whole cycle. Still I didn't dare leave, even to go to my office across the hall. I had to be sure. Everything depended on me.

The boiler ran perfectly, almost to the end of the final cycle, and then suddenly it went dead. I took a deep breath. *Okay, I must have turned a knob too far. Nothing to worry about.* I checked the wiring. Everything looked good. I turned the first knob, then the second. Ensuring I did it exactly right. Again the boiler started, then died. I retraced my steps over and over. No matter what I tried, the result was the same. Finally, I went to my office and got the manual. I followed each instruction to the *T*.

Failure.

It seemed like I was only making the problem worse. The boiler shut down quicker with each attempt I made to fix it. Like it was mocking me. The building was growing colder by the minute. There was nothing more I could do. It was way after midnight. I'd never felt more frustrated and useless. There was no possible way to repair the boiler. Not tonight at least. Come morning, I'd have to call the manufacturer. My only prayer was that my boss wouldn't fire me on the spot. But what were the odds of that? He'd be furious. It would be a miracle if he wasn't. *Yes*, I thought. *A miracle!* That's what I needed. That was my only hope.

I knelt down, head cradled in my hands. "Dear God, I don't know what to do. I need help. Give me the words to say to my boss. Help him understand."

There was a knock on the door. *Who could this be?* I knew the building was empty.

"Who is it?" I said, getting to my feet.

The door opened and in walked a young airman carrying a technician's tool bag, spotless, as if it was being used for the first time. He wore an olive-green uniform, perfectly pressed, open at the collar, cap in hand. His boots, I couldn't help but notice, were shined to a mirror finish. I looked for his name tag, but he didn't have one.

"Mr. Waller, I'm here to get this boiler going," he said. "You can go back to your office and look after the rest of the building. I've got this covered." His voice was strong, so confident that I didn't think to question him. I felt immediately at ease.

"That's great. I really appreciate you coming out." He nodded and began adjusting the knobs on the boiler. I went back to my office and watched the monitor in amazement. The boiler came on and stayed on. Slowly the temperature and the humidity levels began to rise. How had he fixed it so easily? I had to know the answer.

I went back to the boiler room. The airman was standing in the corner. "It just needed some adjusting but it's running fine now," he said. "The run-through with the flight simulators in the morning should be good to go."

"I can't thank you enough," I said. He was halfway through the doorway when it hit me. "I didn't catch your name."

He looked at me over his shoulder and said, "John." I watched him walk down the hallway and out the door. Except for the hum of the boiler the building was silent again. Quiet enough for me to hear John start the engine to his service vehicle. But I heard nothing. Had he walked? It was a good half-mile to the Heat Shop, the department that oversaw all the heating systems for the entire base. I remembered the spotless bag he had carried. Could this really have been his first day? Pretty impressive. I'd definitely make sure to tell his boss.

Later that morning, when the operator came in to take the next shift, I drove over to the Heat Shop. The supervisor was just sitting down with a cup of coffee.

"That new airman, John, the one who got sent over to fix the boiler at the Flight Sim Building last night? He really knows his stuff. I would have never got it going without . . ."

The supervisor looked puzzled. "We don't have an airman in the Heat Shop named John. And I know there were no service calls last night." He paused. "Tom, are you feeling all right? You are turning white as a sheet. You better go home and get some rest."

I said good-bye and stumbled out to my car in a daze. For the longest time I just sat there in the driver's seat, questions flooding my mind. Who was this John? I hadn't imagined him. I knew that without a doubt. But how had he known my name? Or that I had an office. About the critical performance tests for the flight simulators on Monday morning. The boiler. Yes, the boiler. He'd sure saved my bacon. As if he was responding directly to a call for help. But I hadn't . . . Then I remembered: my prayer for a miracle. God had sent me the ultimate repairman, always nearby, ready with the answer, an angel, on call 24–7.

Prayer from a Young Soldier
Laurence Eldred

OKINAWA. A SHIVER PASSED THROUGH ME when we were told it was there our troop transport was headed. The men in my 713th Tank Flamethrowers Battalion stared at one another. The island was the last stepping-stone prior to invading the Japanese mainland. We knew it was going to be bloody. I was a twenty-one-year-old army private. I had no expectation of coming out alive.

We entered Nakagusuku Bay—later called Buckner Bay in honor of our commanding general, Simon Bolivar Buckner Jr.—late morning in early April 1945. Almost immediately the Japanese opened fire.

I was below deck with the rest of my battalion when the battle-stations siren sounded. *This is it*, I thought. Above, we could hear the whine of a squadron of approaching Japanese Zeros, the long-range fighter planes flown by kamikaze crews.

We were part of a convoy. There were several other troop transports—I can't remember how many—as well as a destroyer, a cruiser, and a hospital ship. There was no mistaking why the hospital ship was there.

And then our ship's twin, ninety-millimeter antiaircraft guns opened fire. So did the guns on every other US ship. The noise, the power—I'd never heard anything like it. Never had *imagined* anything like it. It sounded like the world was exploding. I had to see this for myself. Maybe to take some control over my fate. The other guys thought I was crazy. "You'll get yourself killed," one said. He might have been right. But I couldn't stop myself. I couldn't stay below deck a moment longer. *Protect me, Lord*, I prayed, and headed for the companionway stairs.

I climbed to the deck and made my way just beneath those big guns. The sailors who manned them fired at the Zeros with everything they had. There must have been two dozen planes bearing down on the ship like hungry raptors. The sailors kept firing and firing. The planes kept boring in, no more than one hundred feet off the ground.

One plane burst into flames, then pinwheeled into the sea. Then another. And another. Artillerymen on the other ships opened fire too. Plane after plane fell from the sky.

Me, I stood there, transfixed. *It's like a duck hunt*, I thought. *Just like when my older brother and I would head out to the river near our house and take aim at a covey of ducks passing over us.*

For some strange reason, I wasn't afraid. Till one Zero cut through all the artillery fire and aimed straight at us. *It's going to hit us*, I thought. *It's going to destroy the ship.*

The artillerymen didn't flinch. They did the job they were expected to do. I stood there unable to move.

Then I felt something. Something that set me in motion. Two hands, gently but urgently pressing on my back. They pushed me toward the companionway ladder that led below deck. *Who's that?* I wondered, and swiveled my head around.

No one was there.

I paused at the top of the companionway ladder. Again, the two hands. Now they were pushing me down the ladder, as fast as I could go.

I reached the lower deck and stopped, wondering how I had gotten there and why. That's when I heard the boom. A boom that rattled the ship, that exploded in my ears. I shook my head, trying to clear the concussive sound. Alarms were going off everywhere. Sailors raced past me to their posts.

I remained where I was, not that I had any choice. I was too shaken to move. I kept waiting to feel the ship start sinking. But after a few tense minutes, I realized we were okay. I waited a few more minutes, then climbed back up the companionway ladder to the deck.

What struck me was the silence. I couldn't figure what was missing. Then I turned to where the sailors had stood, firing the twin, ninety-millimeter antiaircraft guns.

The men were gone. Out in the water, halfway between our ship and the hospital ship, a Japanese Zero was rapidly sinking. Only its tail section remained afloat.

I blinked, trying to put it all together. A soldier from my unit tapped me on the shoulder. "Man," he said, "were you ever lucky. If you had stayed on deck, you would have been blown to bits."

A shiver ran through me. I'd been protected. Why, I didn't know. But how was with two powerful hands.

Angel at My Door

Paul Tomlinson

IT WAS EARLY SUMMER. The woman who stood at my front door was attractive, tall, well-dressed, and wore a uniform from the local gas company. "I'm here to check your gas furnace," she said with a smile.

"But I didn't call for repairs," I said. I had heard stories of scam artists who wormed their way into homes and got residents to pay for unnecessary repairs.

"I don't do repair work," she clarified. "I'm here to make sure your furnace is safe for the winter. No charge."

No charge? "Okay... but I'm not paying for anything I don't need."

We went downstairs to the furnace. She removed the front cover. "This furnace is filthy," she said. "It must be at least thirty years old. When did you last get it cleaned?"

Oh, so here was the sales pitch. "I suppose you'd want the job?" I asked.

"Any furnace company can do it," she said. "Make sure to get it cleaned before you turn it on. Don't forget."

In October, the weather cooled and I called a heating and air-conditioning company. A man spent hours scrubbing off grime. Then he lit a smoke bomb to check for leaks. White clouds billowed from every vent in the house.

The furnace man looked aghast. "Don't turn this furnace on," he said. "If you do, you won't wake up in the morning."

I got a new furnace installed the next day. Thank God that woman from the gas company came around the neighborhood.

Except she didn't. None of my neighbors received an inspection. The gas company hadn't sent anybody before or since.

Angel in the Mirror
Sally Edwards Danley

"Grammy, when Daddy's not home, his new wife, Estelle, is mean to Melissa. She slaps her face and spanks her. We don't know why. But we don't want her to be our mama anymore."

The voice of the four-year-old made me want to cry. "Grammy" was my best friend, Josie, and I'd gone to Josie's house to help with her three granddaughters for the weekend while her husband, Tom, was working out of town on a construction job.

I'd heard so much about Josie's granddaughters that I had looked forward to helping.

The girls' dad, Peter, was the younger of Josie and Tom's two sons. He and his new wife, Estelle, were on a weekend getaway. It was about an hour after Peter left when little Teena suddenly told of her new stepmother's cruelty.

"Yeah, Grammy," piped up Barby, the youngest, who was three. "An' she spanks 'lissa. I don't like to see my sissy cry." Her tears surfaced as she spoke.

Josie and I were both shocked.

Melissa, five, was walking slowly across the room toward Josie with her head hung low. She remained silent as her sisters spoke. Then she looked up at Grammy, who opened her arms. Melissa crawled onto Josie's lap. Then the other two joined her. I was sitting beside them on the couch. When Barby climbed into my lap, I was delighted in how easily she trusted me.

Melissa had tried not to cry when her sisters reported the abuse. But feeling safe at last, she sobbed in her grandmother's arms. All three sobbed. Josie and I even had tears trickling down our cheeks.

A week earlier, during our routine Saturday breakfast at a local restaurant, Josie had told me that Estelle seemed to be having difficulty adjusting to the girls. She had never had children nor been married. Being a mother to three young, energetic stepdaughters was not easy.

Now, after hearing that report from both girls, Josie was shaken. But she didn't know what to do. A very gentle woman, she was too timid to tell anyone—even Tom.

I was grateful that I was there so she didn't have to carry that emotional load alone.

For the next couple of weeks, more reports spilled out from the younger girls about several other incidents. We determined that Estelle would hit Melissa instead of one of the younger ones who had actually done wrong. None of the girls told their dad. Melissa just accepted the punishment silently.

Josie and I were frustrated because we didn't know how to stop it. I suggested she tell Peter or the authorities. But she didn't want to upset Peter or Tom. She was afraid of them turning against her, especially since she didn't have proof.

Feeling powerless, one Saturday I suggested we pray and ask God to protect the girls. Josie quickly agreed. She grabbed my hand across the table and asked me to pray.

I said, "Lord, Josie and I know You are especially protective of helpless little children. We know You can keep them from harm. So, Lord, we ask You to send a mighty angel to guard and protect little Melissa from Estelle. Thank You, Lord, for stationing that angel in her bedroom."

A week later, Josie and I took Melissa shopping for school clothes. We had left Teena and Barby at home with Tom.

Melissa was so happy to be treated like a big girl. We chatted about the importance of her starting kindergarten the next month. We were three girls out shopping and having fun talking.

The sun was setting when we left the shopping center. As we walked across the huge parking lot toward Josie's car, Melissa stared at the brilliant pole lights.

Suddenly, she said, "That's almost as bright as my angel in the mirror."

Josie and I stopped abruptly. We were shocked with her unexpected comment.

"Oh, do you have an angel lamp, Melissa?" I asked.

"No," she said. "It's a real angel in my big mirror. When I went to bed I used to be really scared. But now at night this beautiful glowing angel is always in the mirror on my dresser. She's so big she fills up the whole mirror. She sings real soft to me and I know she'll keep me safe. She makes it easy to go to sleep."

Josie looked relieved and whispered that she hadn't heard anything from the other girls lately about Melissa being struck.

We drove back to Josie's house, listening to Melissa jabbering happily.

The next week Peter and Estelle separated. Later he told Josie what had happened. One evening he had gone to say good-night to Melissa in her bedroom. When he opened the door, he saw Estelle shaking the child and scolding her in a whisper. He was furious and ordered Estelle out of the room. He soothed his crying child and held her until she relaxed and was ready to sleep.

Peter realized he couldn't trust his girls alone with Estelle anymore. So he asked her to leave that night. His daughters were more important to him than a cruel woman, and eventually the marriage ended.

The girls never said anything else about what had happened after we prayed. We only know Melissa was definitely guarded by an angel. We suspect it had in some way brought Peter into the room at the right time. Regardless, we were thankful for that angel in the mirror.

Comfort in the Waiting Room
Beverly Baker

THERE MUST HAVE BEEN AT LEAST a hundred people crowded into the waiting room outside a lab at the MD Anderson Cancer Center in Houston. All of them—all of *us*—cancer patients or worried family members, like my husband, Mike. Everyone was whispering, filling the room with an eerie hiss. I could see the stricken look in the faces around me, how weak and helpless the disease and the chemo had left them. Some people wore surgical masks, their skin pale. Others had lost their hair. I'd never seen so many people with IVs, in wheelchairs...

That's going to be me, I thought. *I have cancer.* The realization sent a cold chill through me. My hands trembled uncontrollably. I grabbed Mike's arm and took a deep breath. Not long ago in the shower I'd felt a lump under my arm. My doctor confirmed my worst fear after a whirlwind of X-rays and tests. I'd come here for prelab work, my surgery two days away. And after that? What if surgery wasn't enough? *Please, God, help me,* I prayed. But I felt no comfort.

"It will be okay," Mike said. "This is a great hospital. Your surgeon knows what he's doing. You can't lose faith."

How could he be calm? Could he not see everyone around us? This was serious. People died from cancer.

I couldn't bear to think of not being there for Mike, for our four children. I'd just turned fifty. My best years ahead. Or so I'd thought. I cradled my head in my hands. My surgeon was optimistic. I shouldn't be this frightened. But I couldn't calm myself. All I could think about were the weddings I wouldn't cry at, the grandchildren I'd never hold. Who would care for my mother? I'd dreamed of growing old with Mike. I wasn't strong enough to fight. Already I felt weak. What if the doctor was wrong? What if it was too late?

I felt something move at my feet, a rustling sound. I opened my eyes to see a woman kneeling in front of me. She reached out and rested her hand on my knee. *What is she doing?*

She was in her early sixties, wearing a burgundy sweater and navy slacks. She had short brown hair, stylishly cut, but no makeup or jewelry. Through her glasses I gazed back at the kindest, most compassionate hazel eyes I'd ever seen. There was something so comforting about her, despite the strange situation.

Instinctively I placed my hand on hers and she put her free hand on top of mine. Her hands were crisscrossed with veins, slightly rough in places, a mother's hands, hands used to working.

She looked up at me and in a soft, soothing voice said, "I can see how scared you are, dear, but don't worry. You are going to be okay."

Even in the crowded waiting room I heard every word she said. The noise around me was gone, as if she and I were the only people in the room.

She didn't say another word. But her eyes never left mine while she gently stroked my hand. Then she stood up and walked away. I looked to Mike and then back to where the woman had last been standing. But now she wasn't there. I scanned the room but couldn't find her.

"Strange, huh?" I said to Mike.

"What is?"

"The woman at my feet," I said, trying not to sound irritated. What did he think I was talking about?

"I didn't see a woman," Mike said.

I knew I hadn't imagined her. I'd felt her hand. A human touch. Heard her soothing voice. Even now, after she'd gone I felt calm and relaxed, a sense of peace I'd never known before. That couldn't have come from me.

"Mike," I said, "I think I just had a visit from an angel."

Mike took my hand and squeezed it. "You're not alone in this," he said. "That much I know for sure."

Two days later I had my surgery, a lumpectomy. The surgeon said that the tumor was small and intact. It took ten more days to get the results of the lymph node biopsies. It felt like forever, but whenever I got worried I thought of the woman I'd encountered in the waiting room, the comfort of her voice, the warm assurance of her touch.

When the news came that my lymph nodes were cancer free we thanked God for His blessing. I went through chemotherapy and radiation as a precaution against reoccurrence, but I wasn't afraid. I knew Mike was right. I wasn't alone.

Today, almost eleven years later, I remain cancer free. I've seen all of my children graduate from college and I've danced at one of their weddings. I delight daily in my beautiful granddaughter. And no matter what happens there's a peace that never leaves me. A peace given to me by an angel when I needed it most.

My Prayer for the Orange Trees
Carolyn Werly-Wilder

"I've never seen cold weather last so long!" Mom said when I arrived at the family ranch near Mariposa, California. Since Dad died she was on her own up there. Normally she was able to manage the place by herself, but this January had brought unusually frigid weather for California, and she needed my help.

"Don't worry," I told her. "I'll load more wood in the stoves. Then I'll check on the oranges." The small orchard behind the house was our pride and joy. It had weathered many winters—but never one like this. Any temperatures below freezing were incredibly dangerous for both the orange crop and the trees themselves, and the long-range forecast wasn't good. When Mom called and told me the temperature had dipped as low as thirty degrees, I drove right over. "I think it's time to turn on the sprinklers," I said, grabbing a flashlight. The running water caused the air temperature to rise, and even just a few degrees could make all the difference.

Outside I got the system up and running. Water droplets burst across the little field. The orchard was small, but mighty in its own way.

The ranch sat in the foothills of the Sierra Nevada mountains, and citrus trees at this elevation—over one thousand feet—were rare. When my dad's parents had homesteaded here in the early 1900s, they used all the land for cattle grazing.

Then Grandpa noticed the cows had a funny habit of bedding down behind the house in winter. Turned out, this one area was warmer than any other place for miles around. Maybe warm enough to plant some fruit, he thought.

Grandpa worked for years to make the soil more fertile. He grafted the roots of two varieties of oranges—the hardy, cold-resistant Mediterranean Sweet and the delicious Washington Navel—to create his own hybrid. He planted his saplings in spring and, under his care, a field of twenty orange trees flourished. It seemed impossible, but there they were. Our miracle trees.

A sputtering sound from the sprinklers caught my attention. The flow of water petered out and stopped. *Oh no,* I thought. *The pipes must have frozen!* Now what?

I rushed back to the house to tell Mom. "I don't know what to do," I said. "It's so cold, we won't just lose the fruit. The trees could die."

"While you were out, I called my prayer chain at church," Mom said. "Now the orchard is in God's hands." I wished I felt that was enough.

I went back outside. A typical California citrus harvest starts in October, but we held off until February. The cold climate and the long wait made the oranges irresistibly sweet, like candied fruit right off the branch. People came from all over to get a taste of them. I touched the frosty bark of one of the trees. If we picked the oranges now they wouldn't be the same. Plus, harvesting the crop wouldn't save the trees.

Lord, what else can we do? It's only getting colder. One of my favorite scriptures came to mind: "For he will command his angels concerning you to guard you in all your ways." I'd relied on that promise so many times in my life. Could it possibly help me now?

I walked down the line of trees. "Please send angels to protect the orchard," I asked. "Angels with hot breath to lift the frost." I touched an orange on each tree as I walked past. They were hard as ice. I felt overcome with sadness as I walked back to the house. I looked over my shoulder and realized I'd skipped two of the trees off to one side. *I suppose it doesn't really matter . . . .*

Back at the house the thermometer read twenty degrees. How many nights could the trees weather this freeze? It went without saying that the oranges themselves were ruined, but that hardly mattered to me now in the face of losing the very trees they grew on.

For five consecutive nights the temperature fell below freezing. On the morning of the sixth day, the weather report improved. The cold snap was over! Mom and I bundled up and trudged outside to survey the damage. All the native, cold-weather plants around the house were withered and black. My heart buckled at the thought of what our orange trees would look like.

We stepped behind the house. Our miracle trees had never appeared more beautiful, all deep green leaves and bright amber oranges. Every tree in the orchard was well. All except—

"These two trees didn't make it," I said. Their leaves were shriveled up and their trunks frostbitten. The dead oranges had already started to drop off. They were the two trees I'd neglected to touch with my prayer.

I picked an orange off one of the trees that appeared to have made it. The fruit was so cold it made my hand sting. "Cut it open," Mom said. I split the orange in half. The inside practically glowed. It was perfectly healthy. And as sweet as the God who holds our orchard in His hands.

Kelly's Angel

Dee Fleming

MY HUSBAND, DON, AND I pulled into the high school parking lot that cold December afternoon. It had been twenty months since the shootings. Twenty months, and still I could hardly bear to look at that building.

Sometimes it seemed like only twenty minutes since the April day in 1999 when we waited with the hundreds of other frantic parents for our children to make their way through the cordon of police and emergency vehicles surrounding Columbine High School. Some of the kids came out crying, frightened, stunned. Some were rushed from the school in ambulances.

One teacher and twelve students, including our sixteen-year-old Kelly, did not come out. For a day and a half they remained where they had died while investigators pieced together an account of two teenage boys who had fallen into the grip of a terrible evil—the evil that seemed to me to hover still about the place where it happened.

Like most of the others, Kelly was killed in the library, crouching beneath a table as bullets ricocheted through the room. *Just inside those windows!* I thought as Don got out of the car. Right behind that curved steel-and-glass façade. It was too much to bear. I turned my head away, unable to look.

It had been weeks before the examination of the crime scene was complete and police let the families visit the site. It was important to me to see the place where Kelly had tried to hide. I needed to pray at the spot, outlined in white on the floor, kneel where she died. But if I thought actually going to the library would ease its menace, I was wrong. The bullet-scarred walls, the splintered tabletops, a shattered computer screen—violence and hate were still palpable there.

We live just two blocks from the high school, and for a long time I could not even drive by it, taking long, bizarre detours for the simplest errands. But for Don's sake, and for our older daughter, Erin, I had to pick up my life again. And what helped most was remembering how Kelly loved angels.

From the time she was tiny, Kelly and I had shared a special affection for these messengers of God. I can still hear her piping little voice, at age three, reciting the verse on the little guardian angel card my mother had given her:

"Angel of God, my guardian dear

to whom his love commits me here,

ever this day be at my side

to light and guard,

to rule and guide."

Kelly loved that card. I'd often see it on her dresser top or catch sight of it with her schoolbooks. When she was older we would sit together on the sofa and watch *Touched by an Angel*. We never missed an episode. We bought the soundtrack CD, too, and would sing along in the car, just the two of us.

For Kelly and me, angels were our shorthand for "God is near!" And His nearness is what made her such a happy child—a girl who woke in the morning with a smile and literally skipped through the day, blue eyes sparkling, long blonde hair swishing behind her.

That's what gave the library its peculiar horror for me. Kelly was such a gentle, trusting little soul to die amid such evil! I'd given her a poem about angels that she kept in a frame on her bedroom wall. After she died I'd step into her room again and again and read it, lingering over one line especially: "Angels are with you every step of the way and help you soar with amazing grace." I wanted to believe an angel had been beside her that day, with her beneath that table, helping her soar above the terror.

Almost as though they knew I needed them, people sent angel figurines along with their condolences. They came from friends, neighbors, total strangers—china angels, metal angels, wooden angels. An eight-year-old daughter of a friend tried to count the angel images in our house one day and gave up at 175—and every one of those angels whispered to me that Kelly was fine.

Only around the library was I unable to feel comfort. Not that we hadn't tried to exorcise the evil from that place. The school district at first wanted to repair and refurbish the space, but Don and I and the other parents believed that no child should ever again be asked to study there. God brought us together in an organization we called HOPE—Healing of People Everywhere—to raise money for a brand-new library building.

What began as a fund-raising effort among the families was caught up by the whole community, then by the entire nation and even beyond. The new school building was under construction now—Don had driven in that afternoon, as he often did, to check on its progress. "I'll stay in the car," I told him. I'd visited the building site with the other families just a few days earlier.

The new library posed no terrors. It seemed to me a sign of life continuing, life affirmed. It was the presence of the old site that continued to oppress and upset me. I glanced reluctantly at it through the car window.

Its exterior was unchanged, but inside, I knew, nothing was left of the old facility. Architects had come up with a design that preserved the cafeteria on the ground floor, while entirely removing the second floor where the library had been.

The cafeteria now had a spacious atrium feel, bright and light, with a beautiful mural of trees on the high ceiling, drawing the eye upward. Students and faculty of Columbine High School had a space that all could enter without fear. With the other families, we'd see to it that no physical trace of the tragedy remained.

Yet for me, the place still menaced. I turned my back on it and stared the other way out the car window. *I need to know that Kelly's all right, Lord*, I prayed. *I need to know she's happy and at peace.*

Turn around. Look at the building. The nudge didn't come from me. That building was the last thing in the world I wanted to look at. I wrenched my head around . . . and blinked in astonishment.

Something bright was moving across those upper windows! Something shimmering and glowing, gliding slowly past the glass exactly where the old library had been. Openmouthed I stared while the unmistakable figure of an angel hovered over that second story. Wings, radiant hair, flowing garment—no artist could have rendered a heavenly messenger of comfort more gloriously.

I sat awestruck, seeing, yet scarcely believing. *Even here, even here! Your angel was here with Kelly, just as You are with her always and forever.*

How long did the vision last—fifteen seconds? However brief the time on a clock, I knew the angel had given me a lifetime of assurance. In the midst of all the evil that ever was and ever will be, God is present. God is with us. God is stronger.

Heaven-sent

Bernadine Paulson

"Now, Bernie, don't go outside alone—not even to get the mail," my doctor warned over the phone. "These North Dakota winters are dangerous. If you slip, who will be there to help you?"

I appreciated his concern, but . . . not even for the mail? At sixty-one, I wasn't as sure on my feet as I used to be, but I was no invalid. He was right about one thing though. I was often alone. My husband and I had a brood of fourteen, but they had all flown the nest—and the icy winters of our small town. While my husband was working, I was by myself.

I looked outside. Over a foot of snow blanketed the neighborhood. Our driveway was a steep slope and needed to be shoveled. *Okay, Lord,* I prayed. *Walk with me.*

Slowly, I trudged down to the mailbox and got my mail. *Ha! There!* Triumphant, I turned back up the slope.

My rubber boots lost their grip. Envelopes flew. Sliding helplessly on the ice, I spun around, just barely managing to hug the mailbox. I caught my breath.

"Here—let me help you." A tall, dark-haired man, wearing only a T-shirt and overalls, stood beside me. Who in his right mind would dress like that in this weather? But I accepted his offer.

He held me gently by the elbow, guiding me up the slope, step by step, to my front door. "Thank you," I said, glancing down at my snowy boots, stomping them on the welcome mat. "Aren't you cold like that?" He didn't answer.

I looked up. He wasn't standing beside me. I was alone. Only one trail of footprints led up the snowy driveway to my front door.

Angels on Board
Vesta-Nadine Severs

I WAS DRIVING ON THE HIGHWAY with my daughter and grandchildren when a red pickup truck barreled down a ramp into my lane. I swerved too late—

Smash! The pickup hit our right rear door. We spun and came to a stop in a patch of wet grass. The children screamed, then burst into tears.

"*Shh,*" I said, trying to comfort them and check for injuries at the same time. Besides minor scrapes, bumps, and bruises, they were all okay physically. But they were still badly frightened. They couldn't stop crying.

"It's all right," their mom and I assured each one—except four-year-old Stephen. He didn't need reassurance. He was perfectly calm. He hadn't cried or screamed at all.

"Wasn't it good that the angels held our doors shut?" he said.

"Yes, dear," I said, as my daughter and I did another check for injuries just to be safe. I barely heard what Stephen said.

But the next day he was still talking about those angels.

"I saw four angels in white robes," he explained.

He described them surrounding the outside of the car when we got hit, like the angels were protecting us.

The adult Stephen stands by his story. He tells it vividly to this day. He remembers the four mighty angels who were with us during that terrifying accident. I didn't see the angels that day, but no doubt they were there.

A Guy Named Andy

Timothy J. Burt

I WAS WALKING PAST the Denver Mint on a nearly perfect evening in early September. I had just eaten my one meal of the day at a local burger place and was casually wandering back to the Episcopal church where I had stayed in the basement the previous three nights with other street people, indigents, and runaways.

At nineteen years old, I'd left home one night near the end of August and hitchhiked from New Jersey to Colorado. I'd had enough of the long history of constant turmoil, criticism, and abuse in my family. One night I simply could take no more and escaped. With fifty dollars in my pocket, a sleeping bag, and my backpack full of clothes and snacks, I left. I planned to go to Steamboat Springs and be a ski bum.

God had other plans.

A stranger approached me in front of the Denver Mint.

"Hi, there," I said.

"And how are you this evening, my brother?" he responded.

Within moments he correctly assessed that I'd not had much to eat that day, and he insisted that I go with him to get some food. I resisted but he insisted.

His name was Andy Witherspoon, and he told me that he worked construction in the Denver area and that he spent a lot of time helping street kids and runaways. He said he lived outside of town somewhere and that, since he gave away most of the money he made, everything he owned was in the modest gym bag he carried.

Andy was a short, slight, middle-aged black man, and I wondered how he was able to handle construction.

Andy seemed to intuitively know a lot about me, but I guessed since he spent a lot of time with runaways, there must be some commonality. He understood my discomfort with the contrast between my abusive home situation and my new-found faith, and he did not condemn me for leaving, but he was concerned about the distance I'd come and the resentments I harbored.

While we ate, he suggested that I go home and reconcile with my parents. This little man who had never finished ninth grade strongly recommended continuing my college education, even though I didn't see the point.

Night fell and Andy instructed me to watch how he dealt with a panhandler. Only six or seven minutes later he sent the man away without what he thought he needed: money. Instead, Andy spoke respectfully into the man's heart and addressed his real need, which was spiritual. The man walked away smiling after only a few minutes of interaction with Andy Witherspoon. Such was the wisdom and love this man exuded.

Then Andy and I met a rich kid from Indiana who was living in an expensive Denver hotel. Andy treated him with the same respect and dignity he'd shown the panhandler thirty minutes before. I realized that none of my professors at college had the wisdom or knowledge of this gentle man. No one I'd ever met spoke like Andy Witherspoon.

He suggested that the guy from Indiana let me stay in his hotel room for the night, and the guy agreed. I didn't need to go back to the Episcopal church, since everything I owned was on my back. I appreciated a clean, safe, quiet room that night and never thought I'd see Andy again.

The next morning I awoke and left the hotel early. Two days before, I'd helped a couple of young pastors move some equipment and theatrical lighting.

They had invited me to a special Sunday morning musical at the First Church of the Nazarene.

I enjoyed the production and was invited to stay for the potluck lunch afterward. Afterward, one of the families at the potluck dropped me off near the bus station. I planned to take the next bus to Steamboat Springs and do my ski-bum thing.

But God had other plans.

Because I'd gone to church that morning, I'd missed the early bus to Steamboat. The next bus didn't leave until Sunday night. I suddenly had lots of time to explore or just relax on another perfect afternoon in early September.

I stretched out on the grass in the middle of Denver's largest park and closed my eyes. I didn't even look up when I thought I heard my name because, after all, no one knew me and I was all alone in this huge park.

The voice again clearly called "Tim!" and I sat up and looked around. It was Andy Witherspoon! He had not been there when I'd lain down only two or three minutes earlier. I told him all about the church musical, my plans for Steamboat, the schedule for the next bus, and what I thought my future would look like.

This time while we talked, I insisted that he go with me for something to eat—my treat this time. We found a local chicken place and sat together talking again.

Andy did all he could to convince me to go home. He said two wrongs didn't make a right; and he told me again to go home, be reconciled with my parents, and return to school.

His words hit me hard. Truth was having an impact. God broke me right there, right then. I couldn't stop crying, sitting in a public eatery with a short, middle-aged man. I kept turning my face toward the wall as Andy's wisdom and care challenged my plans and assuaged nearly twenty years of hurts and fears and criticism.

Andy knew that the ski-bum lifestyle would take me away from my newfound faith in God. He also knew that I had not received God's message the previous night. I told Andy I would not go to Steamboat—I would head home.

We must have said good-bye after finishing our meal, but all these years later I simply can't remember. Instead of the 7:30 PM bus to Steamboat, I bought a ticket to Omaha, Nebraska—as far as I could go on my remaining money.

Who was Andy Witherspoon? He just "happened" to appear at two critical points in this journey with guidance from God specifically for me, and he claimed to live outside of Denver someplace. But he had no car to get back and forth, and he claimed to have only one change of clothes and a few incidentals in his gym bag.

Andy claimed to work in the construction industry, which is usually reserved for rough-and-tumble guys who are not Andy's diminutive size and don't possess his gentle character. And he gave away most of his money?

I'm reminded of Hebrews 13:2 (NIV): "Do not forget to show hospitality to strangers, for by so doing some people have shown hospitality to angels without knowing it".

It was 11:30 PM in Omaha, and I began hitchhiking, headed east. I hitchhiked the rest of the way home and finished college. The life journey God arranged for me ultimately led to graduate school, a vocation as a counselor, and volunteering as a hospital chaplain. I feel privileged to be involved in these ministries and to know that God is using me to influence others—in a small way—as Andy impacted me so long ago.

The Angel's Presence
Nancy Moore

NEAR THE END OF SUMMER, I had flown from Ohio to the suburbs of Philadelphia to help two friends: one, recovering from carpal tunnel surgery on both hands; the other, from shoulder surgery. During my stay, I developed severe chest pain and was rushed to the ER. The diagnosis was an acute gall bladder attack, complicated by pancreatitis, and I was hospitalized for two weeks before becoming strong enough for surgery. After the operation, my surgeon reported that two of my liver ducts were fused. I was taken to the gloomy Radiology Department located in the basement of the hospital for two sessions where dye was forced through my liver with what looked like a large turkey baster, but it failed to make a difference.

As far as I was concerned, those painful sessions were worse than the surgery itself. The surgeon then informed me that she suspected possible cancer. I would need to have a biopsy in six weeks or so after returning home.

I remember receiving this news while watching a TV program about breast cancer, and feeling numb. Suddenly, I seemed to be facing the possible end of my life, with so much unfinished. Within the past year and a half, my husband and I had moved from Iowa to Ohio; my husband had taken a new position in clinical prenatal genetics at Children's Hospital in Columbus; my daughter prepared to leave for college; my son entered his junior year in high school. Because we were still somewhat new in the neighborhood, we did not yet have close friends or a familiar church or extended family on whom to call. It had been a stressful time, and now I was facing a fearful prospect.

With a tube extending from my surgical incision, I flew home to wait the six weeks. We contacted an oncologist in Columbus who would do a brush biopsy, and on the selected date, I was to appear at Riverside Hospital at 7:00 AM. A nurse asked my husband to remain in the waiting room, and led me to a small changing cubicle, where I was instructed to put on a gown and cap.

The room was cold, as is typical in hospital facilities; time passed slowly. The clock on the wall now said seven thirty. I felt suspended; spiritually, I was "holding my breath." It was difficult to think ahead to the possibilities. My only prayer was a silent "Help, Lord."

Suddenly, I felt a warm blanket being placed around my shoulders and a wonderful peace enveloping my mind and body. I had not been given any medication or tranquilizers; no one had entered the room. I knew this was God's presence, and sat there delighted, enjoying His comfort and the "blanket" His angel had brought me.

When the attendant came to escort me upstairs, I ascended cheerfully and unafraid, met with the anesthesiologist, then climbed onto the table to be put to sleep. Waking up in recovery, I felt the same warm blanket, only this time, it was placed by a nurse who told me that there was no sign of cancer and that I could return home after resting. The tube was removed from my side, and I was free to go.

In my time of need and fear, God sent His angels to surround me with their warmth and envelop me with their peace.

Our Angel Wears Purple

Linda S. Clare

THE GREAT RECESSION OF 2008 was a hard time for many, including my family. First, my husband lost his job. I worked, but didn't make enough to cover our needs and those of our two young sons. We lost our home to foreclosure. And now we were weeks late on the rent for our apartment too.

I found a second part-time job in one of the last remaining independent Christian bookstores in Southern California. I didn't tell a soul about our latest financial problem. With two little boys to raise and two jobs, I didn't have much time for anything. Both my husband's and my families lived in different states, and our church friends struggled to keep their own lives afloat. We were broke and on our own. And the rent was more than overdue. The landlord had run out of patience. I dreaded the seventy-two-hour notice that was sure to appear on our door soon.

I was worn out from juggling my jobs and family, but I jumped at the chance at a Saturday shift. What an answer to prayer—even if I wouldn't be paid for it until too late.

I tried to live the things I taught my children—that angels watch over us—but this time I felt as if I'd already dashed my foot against a stone. As the hours ticked by, that stone felt more and like an asteroid. A killer asteroid, ready to smash our world to smithereens.

Questions tumbled through my mind: Who could I call for help? What could I sell? Would the property manager give us just a little more time?

Time was the one thing I didn't have.

Saturday morning, my two boys sat at the table, coloring as I dressed for work. "Mommy," seven-year-old Nathan said. "Do you like my picture?"

I smiled at his crayon drawing. "That's great."

Four-year-old Christian, always serious, gazed up at me, sunshine forming what looked like a halo over the crown of his wispy blond hair. "Mom," he said. "God says angels hafta bear us up, 'member?" He smiled that angelic smile of his. "Here's our angel." He handed me his drawing. In it, an angel dressed in purple flew above a crude drawing of a house.

I knelt beside him. "Why did you make the angel purple, sweetie?"

My son looked at me as if I had missed the point. "Cuz," he said matter-of-factly, "our angel always wears purple."

"Really?" I pinned his drawing to the refrigerator. "Mommy has to go now." I hugged both boys hard and long.

By the time I got to work, I was almost in tears. How would I explain eviction to my children? I prayed for help, then put on a smile and walked up the store's main aisle to unlock the front door. Surrounded by Bibles and encouraging books, I felt defeated. And God felt far away.

As I neared the entrance, a woman, dressed in royal purple from head to toe, stood outside. She paused at the glass doors, dropped what looked like a long white envelope, and hurried away. I quickly turned the key to the main door. "Wait!" I called. "You dropped something! Wait!"

I picked up the envelope and waved it as I continued to shout, hoping she would hear me and stop. But the purple-clad figure disappeared. When I reached the corner, she was nowhere in sight.

I trudged back to the bookstore, where several coworkers now stood with puzzled expressions. I briefly told them what happened and shook my head, sad that someone would be missing the letter. "I just hope it wasn't something they really needed."

I turned over the envelope and gasped. Written across it in a flowing hand was my name. Nothing else. My coworkers urged me on. "Open it!" I pulled the flap open and removed the contents.

I inhaled sharply. Tucked inside the slip of paper, a green stack of money peeked out. "Oh my goodness!" I looked closer. The bills were all hundreds.

Now I cried tears of joy. Crowded around me, my coworkers asked if I knew who might be responsible. No one had seen anyone dressed in purple in the store. Finally one worker pointed to the paper wrapped around the cash. "What's it say?" she asked.

I unfolded it and read: "For He shall give His angels charge over you, to keep you in all your ways, in their hands they shall bear you up, lest you dash your foot against a stone" (Psalm 91:11–12).

My fingers shook and an eerie sensation crawled up my spine. I counted the money—exactly what we needed for our rent, late fee and all. "Thank God," was all I could say. The image of my son's purple angel floated in my mind.

As far as I know, the person who delivered that envelope never came back to the bookstore or identified herself. But soon after, my husband found a new job. Without that envelope, we might not have kept a roof over our heads. And without Christian's purple angel drawing, I may have chalked it up to coincidence.

Our angel, who always wears purple, had truly given us a hand.

One should not stand at the foot of a sick person's bed,

because that place is reserved for the guardian angel.

—JEWISH FOLK SAYING

CHAPTER 3

Angels in Disguise

"I am sending an angel ahead of you to guard you along the way and to bring you to the place I have prepared."

—EXODUS 23:20 (NIV)

My Blue Angel
Katie Bailey Randolph

BLUEBIRDS WERE ALWAYS A SOURCE of joy for my husband, Pete, and me. We loved to watch them in our yard, building their nests in the many bluebird boxes Pete had built to accommodate them. But after Pete's death from heart failure, I had no interest in bluebirds or anything else. I was all alone, and my loneliness consumed me.

"Come look at this!" my daughter called from the kitchen a few days after the funeral. "Come see this silly bluebird!"

I stayed on the couch. The yard was full of birds in August. What could be so special about this one? Kristi came to me in the living room. "Mom, there's just something about this bird you have to see."

I followed her to the kitchen, expecting to see a bluebird perched on one of the boxes or maybe the birdbath. Instead I found him on the screen itself. He turned his bright blue head this way and that, peering into the house as if he was looking for somebody.

"Have you ever seen a bluebird do that?" Kristi said.

"I've never seen one this big," I said. He wouldn't even fit in a bluebird box. With his peach-colored chest puffed out proudly he reminded me of Pete himself. The bird flew to the banister of the porch, then back to the screen door.

One, two, three times. Then he flew up to the flagpole beside the birdbath and just sat.

Pete would have loved him, I thought. It was strange to be watching the bird without him. Pete and I had been inseparable since we got married in 1958. We spent even more time together after our retirement, sitting on the porch, cooking dinner, working on craft projects. Now, what did I have left?

Kristi fixed lunch but I couldn't eat. I could hardly look at the kitchen table, the place where Pete and I had shared our morning prayer each day. I went back to the couch.

Before I knew it, Kristi was calling me again. "Now's he's out by the garage," she said.

Her husband, Keith, had backed Pete's pickup into the driveway while he swept out the garage. The bluebird perched on the truck's open window, looking at the front seat as if seeing someone there. He flew inside to the backseat, then to the front, then flew to the window of Pete's workshop.

"It's like he's visiting all the places that belonged to Dad," Kristi said.

"Strange coincidence," I said. Those places reminded me of my husband, but whatever the bird's reasons for sitting in those places, they had nothing to do with my husband.

By the time I went to sleep that night I'd forgotten all about the bird. So I had no idea what was banging on the screen the next morning until I was face-to-face with him. Once again he flew to the porch banister and back three times. Then he took his spot on the flagpole.

For the rest of the summer and well into the fall, the bird was a daily visitor. Every morning he greeted me at the screen door; every afternoon he sat on the flagpole. Somehow his presence made me feel less alone. Maybe I still took my meals standing at the counter because I couldn't face Pete's empty chair at the table, but at least my bluebird was watching over me. He gave me something to look forward to every morning, and something happy to talk about with friends and family. "What do you call him?" my niece asked me.

"I just call him my Blue Angel," I said. God used a raven and a dove to speak to Noah. Why couldn't He have sent a bluebird to comfort me?

One day in December I caught sight of myself in the mirror. Months of avoiding the kitchen table had left me thin and tired-looking. Even my hair looked scraggly. It was time for me to start taking care of myself. I made an appointment with my hairdresser, Retha.

It was a trek to the salon, but I'd been with her a long time. "I need a cut and a perm," I told Retha when I sat down in her chair.

Retha tied a smock around me and stopped. "What's that?" She pointed out the door of the salon to the street. Something round and blue was perched on Retha's SUV outside. It was my bluebird! There was no mistaking him at that size. He stayed on the SUV throughout my entire appointment and was back home to greet me the next morning as usual.

As I got stronger, my bluebird took some time off. Sometimes he didn't visit for a couple of days at a time. But he was there when I needed him. Like on Valentine's Day when he surprised me at my bedroom window.

One challenge still remained: the breakfast table. I still hadn't so much as pulled out a chair. *Today's the day,* I thought as I got up one morning. I made a cup of coffee and took a seat opposite Pete's empty place. Instinctively I stretched my hand across the table, reaching for Pete's hand to say the morning blessing.

All my months of progress vanished. I was alone again, and the pain overwhelmed me. "How could You take him from me?" I yelled to the empty kitchen. "Why isn't Pete here with me?" I pounded the table and cried, barely aware of where I was and what I was doing. All I knew was how much I hurt.

Then something caught my attention. Something banging on the storm door. I opened my eyes to see my bluebird knocking just as he'd done that first day, his bright peach chest rising and falling as if he'd flown to me in a rush, his little heart beating under his feathers. "I'm here!" he seemed to say. "You're not alone. I'm here."

I'm not alone, I thought. I had my Blue Angel. What was more, I had God.

Later that spring, my bluebird visited me for the last time. But his message remains safe in my heart: I am never alone.

The Mangy Angel

Esther L. Vogt

COLD MARCH SHOWERS PELTED MY FACE as I stepped from the warmth of the church and threaded my way across the lot toward the parsonage.

Thursday evening's meeting of the women's missionary society had finally closed, and as the pastor's wife, I was the last to leave.

My husband had gone to a general conference in Detroit, and the children and I were alone. I half-expected to find the parsonage cloaked with night, for the hour was late and the children should have been in bed hours ago.

Letting myself in quietly, I was surprised to find the kitchen light still burning. Ted, our oldest, his dark head bent over his books, was studying at the table. He looked up as I came in.

"H'lo, Mom. Wet out, isn't it?"

"It's a wild night, all right," I said wryly, peeling off my dripping coat and boots. He went back to his homework.

As I turned to leave the kitchen I looked down. Then I gasped. Our huge mangy dog lay stretched out at Ted's side!

"Ted! What's Brownie doing in the house?" I demanded. "You know he's never stayed inside before!"

Ted glanced up from his book and shrugged. "Why, he just wanted in so I let him in. Then I decided I might as well bring my homework down here."

Brownie wanted in! That, in itself, was utterly incongruous. For that matter, so was everything else about that dog.

Black, brown, and smelly—and of undetermined breed—he had wandered to the parsonage one day and simply decided to stay. He adopted our family and was fiercely protective of us in every way. In fact, he loved us so much that he wanted to be where we were. Yet, once we'd let him into the house, he developed a peculiar claustrophobic streak. He would race in terror from window to door to window until we'd let him out. No amount of bribing or petting could persuade Brownie to remain indoors. Even the dreary *drip-drip* of rain from the eaves failed to lure him inside. He preferred the most inclement outdoor weather to being enclosed.

Until now.

There he was, lying calmly beside Ted in the kitchen like a very ordinary house dog.

I remembered his previous fierce possessiveness of us. Our large, redbrick parsonage sprawled comfortably on a big grassy plot behind the church and opposite the public school. Children often cut across the church property and through our yard when hurrying to and from school. We didn't mind. In fact, they were our friends. Against our better judgment, we often had report cards thrust at us even before parents saw them.

That is, until the dog came. He growled threateningly at anyone who dared cross our yard. Yet Brownie always came when I called him off.

Still, with people dropping in at our parsonage at all hours of the day, I was afraid some day I wouldn't get him called off in time.

I tried desperately to find another home for him, but with no success. Once I even called the Humane Society.

"Sure, lady," they said. "We'll get him. But you gotta catch him and shut him up for us."

Shut Brownie up? Impossible! One might as well try to imprison a victim of claustrophobia in an elevator! Until a better solution presented itself, he would have to remain with us.

And that's how things stood that wild, stormy night I came home from church.

Shaking my head at Brownie's strange behavior, I went down to the basement to bolt the door that leads to the outside. I came back up directly and retired to the living room with the paper.

Ted already had gone up to bed, and I decided to turn in too. The dog still lay on the kitchen floor, his shaggy head resting on his front paws.

Better put Brownie out first, I thought as I entered the kitchen to lock the back door. Rain still drummed steadily against the windows.

But when I tried to get the dog out of the door, he refused to budge. I wheedled; I coaxed. I pushed and pulled. He remained stationary.

Going to the refrigerator, I took out a chunk of meat and tried to bribe him to the door by dangling it in front of him. He still refused to move.

With a bewildered sigh I picked up his hind end, yanked him toward the door, and out of it. Like quicksilver, his front end slid back in!

I grabbed his front end, and the back was in. His four feet seemed like a baker's dozen. Stubborn, determined, yet somehow placid. Talk about Balaam's donkey—I knew exactly how Balaam felt!

Should I call Ted to help me? No, the hour was late and Ted needed his sleep. I decided to shut all the doors to the kitchen and leave the dog inside. Then I went wearily to bed.

The next morning the dog reverted to his true nature and frantically tore out of the house.

A puzzled frown ribbed my forehead as I went down to the basement to turn on the furnace. What had made Brownie behave so strangely? Why had he been determined to remain in the house this one particular night? I shook my head. There seemed to be no answer.

When I reached the bottom of the stairs, I felt a breath of cold, damp air. Then a queer, slimy feeling swept over me. The outside door was open! Was someone in the basement?

After the first wave of panic had drained from me, my reasoning returned.

Someone had gone out of the basement!

Limp with the reality of that fact, I looked around. The windows were as snug and tight on the inside as ever. Whoever had gone out of that door had been in when I had gone down to bolt it the night before! He apparently had heard my unsuccessful attempts to put the dog out and knew he had to come up through the kitchen and face the dog—or go out the door he had come in earlier.

That smelly, stray pooch had known this, and God had used him to keep us safe. Why didn't he growl or bark? I don't know. Maybe he knew he didn't have to.

I had always believed that God has definite work for His holy angels, and that as His child I could lay claim to the verse in Hebrews 1:14 (KJV): "Are they [angels] not all ministering spirits, sent forth to minister for them who shall be heirs of salvation?"

But His "ministering spirit" had taken a peculiar form that wild, stormy night. Instead of glorious, dazzling wings, the Lord had given our guardian angel four stubborn, mangy feet!

Rescue Psalm 91

Dewayne Parish

OKLAHOMA WAS MY NEW HOME now that I was retired from my pastoral work, but as my wife, Ann, and I watched the news one night, I felt more like we were living in Egypt during the time of the ten plagues. "Another hailstorm," I groaned when we saw the warning scroll by at the bottom of the TV screen.

"Oh no!" Ann said.

I looked up sadly, thinking of our roof. Just that afternoon I'd admired it gleaming in the sun. It ought to gleam—it was practically brand-new. Our third new roof in four years, in fact. Each one had been destroyed by brutal Oklahoma hail driven by raging wind. Chunks of ice the size of softballs had dinged the shingles, smashed the vents, and destroyed the guttering. *Not again,* I thought. *Please.*

"A hailstorm is on its way toward Oklahoma City," the weatherman confirmed. According to the weather map, we had forty-five minutes until it was right on top of us.

There was nothing more we could do to prepare. We'd already bought the strongest roof we could find. Once that was in place, I'd anointed the home with oil and prayed over the whole parameter of our property, asking God to send angels to protect it. I watched the rest of the news and checked the clock. Thirty minutes to go before our new roof and my prayers would be put to the test.

I flipped to another TV station, hoping to hear that the storm had changed direction, but it was bearing down ever closer. Twenty minutes. Ten. It was time to bring out the big guns. "I'm going to pray Psalm Ninety-one," I told Ann. I stepped outside the front door. Heavy gray clouds filled the night sky to the northwest. I could already hear the hail coming, hitting everything in its path. I recited from memory: "I dwell in the secret place of the most high and abide under the shadow of the Almighty. I say of the Lord, You are my refuge and my fortress; my God in Whom I trust."

The storm advanced like an invading army, the clouds rolling across the sky above our heads. Hail pelted the roof. Ann walked out to stand with me. "You will deliver us from the snare of the fowler and the deadly pestilence." I imagined the Angel of the Lord spreading His wings out over our property. That would protect us for sure. "You will cover us with Your feathers, and under Your wings shall we trust."

By now I was practically shouting over the storm. The sky was so dark I could barely see anything very clearly. But out in the yard, something dropped from that sky. Not hail, birds. Great big birds, gray and white, with black heads and wingspans three feet across. "I've never seen such a bird," Ann said.

Nor had I. A whole flock descended on our lawn, perhaps a hundred or more. The birds landed on the grass, covering every inch. They tucked their heads under their wings for cover. The hail stopped. The storm moved off. The world went quiet. The birds untucked their heads from their wings. Together they flew off into the sky. Ann and I went back inside. We decided that tomorrow would be soon enough to assess the damage.

The next morning dawned bright and sunny. "Let's do this together," Ann said. We stepped into the yard.

"I don't believe it," I said. Our roof gleamed in the sun, looking brand-new. Not a ding or a missing shingle. The gutters were sound. Even the vegetable garden was untouched. I could see I'd be giving out the number of our roofer to my neighbors. And I had a very good Book I'd highly recommend, as well.

Making the Rounds
Peggy Frezon

I HUDDLED IN THE VINYL CHAIR near the foot of the hospital bed. That man lying there, pale and still, monitors blinking all around him, oxygen tube clamped to his nose—I barely recognized him. How could that be Mike, the husband I'd relied on for thirty-one years? My take-charge guy was battling multiple blood clots in his lungs that had debilitated his body. The doctor said the worst was over. Now we just had to be patient. But I'd made myself sick with worry, spending my days at the hospital and night after sleepless night at home, scared and completely on my own. For the first time in my life, I had no one to depend on.

We were one of those couples who did everything together. At breakfast we did the daily crossword puzzle, sharing a pen. We went together to the gym, where we climbed aboard adjacent treadmill machines, plugged in our ear buds, and watched the same show on TV. When Mike tapped me on the shoulder and pointed to the screen, I always knew exactly what he was thinking. Mike was my rock. *Lord, please help him get better. I feel all alone without him.* A strange sound came from the hospital corridor. A sharp *click-click-click-click* on the linoleum floor drew nearer till it stopped outside Mike's room. I did a double take. A dog loomed in the doorway.

I recognized the breed by his distinctive black-and-white coat highlighted by rust-colored markings—a Bernese mountain dog. The special collar distinguished him as a therapy dog. I gazed at Mike, awake but dazed. I'd been a dog lover all my life, but what could a therapy dog possibly do to help my husband? The dog seemed to read my thoughts. He had a job to do and he got to it. Purposefully, he stepped into the room, handler in tow. I sat quietly watching this well-trained beauty. *Maybe petting the dog's soft fur will give Mike some small comfort.*

As the dog headed toward Mike's bedside, he suddenly stopped. He padded over to my chair and looked into my eyes. With that, the dog nudged his head against my waist, as if asking for a hug. I put my arms around him and buried my face into his thick, velvety fur till I felt the gentle pulsing of his heart. *I am here*, its rhythm seemed to say.

My whole body relaxed. My stress lifted away. Mike smiled from the bed. The dog let me hold him for as long as I needed to. When I finally released him, he put his paw on my knee and looked up at me. I turned to his handler. "How did he know that I was the one who needed him?"

"Gabriel always knows," she said.

I stroked the dog's neck. Gabriel. My angel dog. The Lord knew how to soothe me. He'd keep me strong while my husband regained his health. On that I could depend.

My Coyote Guide
Velia Hilderbrand

BURGA, MY FIFTY-POUND ROTTWEILER, jumped out of the pickup truck when we got to Boynton Canyon in Sedona, our go-to spot for a late afternoon stroll. "This might be our last walk for a while, Burga," I said as I led her to our favorite trail. I was scheduled for foot surgery the next day and overwhelmed with worries. Would things be worse than the doctor initially thought? Would I fully recover use of my foot? Would the surgical staff be well rested before the operation? My fears were out of control!

When Burga and I got closer to our usual trail, we found a group of young worshipers gathered at the threshold, heads bowed in prayer. I didn't want to disturb them.

"Come on, Burga, we'll explore a new path today." She hesitated. Burga was very sensitive to potential danger and was quick to alert me if she suspected any threat whatsoever. "It's okay, girl," I assured her. "We won't go very far."

My promise put her at ease and we headed off. *I wish something could calm me as easily,* I thought. I'd bowed my head many times in the days leading up to this operation, asking for God's loving reassurance but so far, to no avail.

There should've been plenty here to take my mind off my troubles—towering red buttes, deep crimson cliff walls, desert gardens decorated with agave cacti and Arizona sycamore trees. As Burga and I covered new territory, I tried to strip away the anxiety and enjoy the scenery. But today my worries had too strong a hold.

I'd lost track of how long we'd been walking when Burga stopped short.

"What's the matter, girl?"

I looked around, surprised at how disoriented I felt. We'd never been any-where near this part of the canyon before. I surveyed the area for other hikers, but we were all alone. I listened for road traffic. Silence. The sun shifted shadows over the edges of the sandstone rocks. Night was coming. All kinds of wild animals lurked in the canyon. Bears, bobcats, coyotes…

Panic rose in me. Even my fears about my operation paled in comparison. We were lost!

"God, please guide us out of here."

My first thought was to head back the same way we came, but we had changed trails too many times during our hike. I couldn't fathom the way out if I tried. The sun was quickly settling behind the canyon landscape, and crickets were tun-ing up for the evening. I had to act fast. I took a deep breath and considered the forked path before us. I led Burga to the left. *I hope this is the way out.…*

I took a few steps and patted Burga, reassuring her before I looked up—

Less than fifteen feet away a coyote stood in our path, its eyes fixed on us. Burga and I froze in place. I averted my eyes from the coyote's stare, not wanting the animal to feel challenged. I tightened my hold on Burga's leash, expecting her to react. I waited, gripping the leash with both hands, dreading an animal fight with no one here to help me. But Burga remained calm. Here she was, face-to-face with a coyote, acting as if she didn't even see him. Was *I* seeing things? I glanced over at the wild animal—untamed, in its natural habitat—undisturbed by Burga's presence. Holding its position in the middle of the trail we were headed down, the coyote watched us closely, waiting. I couldn't believe these animals weren't lung-ing at one another, and we weren't going to stick around to find out why.

Okay...we'll just go to the right. "Come on, girl," I whispered. With my eyes steady on the coyote, I cautiously sidestepped toward the path to our right. I wasn't sure where it led, but I knew it was safer than passing by that coyote.

As we moved right, the coyote moved alongside us. I drew Burga's leash in. The coyote stopped and stared at us.

Now what? I questioned the wild animal's motives, but in that same moment I felt compelled to fall in step beside it.

Walk with a coyote?

The idea seemed crazy but I did it, Burga at my opposite side. Dusk introduced the night, the canyon, quiet. I felt surrounded by peace, protected. The coyote beside us, but at a safe distance, glanced over at us every few meters, making sure we were still in step. As we traveled together I looked down at Burga, then to the coyote. Each remained indifferent to the other's presence.

Soon the quiet of the canyon carried the sounds of traffic. We were nearing the canyon's entrance! All three of us exited the trail onto the hard surface road. I spotted my pickup truck in the distance. Burga and I broke out into a run. Halfway to the truck, I looked over my shoulder. The coyote stood still in the fading dusk light, watching.

It wasn't until it was all over that I was able to fully digest what had transpired. Burga hadn't seen that coyote. My mind toyed with an idea: Was that really a coyote or was it an angel? An angel meant for only me to see? Years later I still don't have the answer, but I know what I believe.

That walk in the canyon sent me a message loud and clear. No matter what fears I get lost in, God will be right there beside me, to guide me safely through.

Our Very Own Dog for a Day

Joanne Begane

I STARED AT THE ADORABLE PUPPY splayed out on the grass by our pool, his coat glowing in the sun. How could I have been so irresponsible? Tonight, when my husband came home from work, we would return this puppy to the shelter.

I'd made a terrible mistake. Earlier, I brought my son Stevie along with me to run some errands in town. We passed a pet adoption booth, and Stevie laid eyes on the big, red golden retriever. My son fell hard. "Mom, please!" he begged. Before I knew it, I'd signed the adoption papers and was cradling the dog in my arms. When my husband called from work, he wondered if I'd lost my mind.

"We can't take on a big commitment right now," he said.

I'd already explained to Stevie, now happily playing with his two young cousins who were staying with us for the afternoon. Stevie and Bryan, the same age, splashed in the pool, while I settled in the shade with Thomas, still just a baby. Our dog for a day lounged close by.

"Boys, play in the grass till I come back," I called when I felt Thomas's wet diaper. I watched them run around the yard, then brought the baby inside to change him.

Ruff! A shrill bark at the window startled me. I looked up in alarm. *Ruff!* The puppy ran back and forth like a mad dog!

I bolted outside. Stevie stood by the pool, alone. "Bryan!" I yelled. There in the deep end was my nephew, flailing his arms. I dove in and pulled him to the ladder. My nephew was safe.

The baby went down for a nap, and the bigger boys played inside for the rest of the day. We returned the dog to the shelter that evening, as planned, where he didn't stay long before finding his forever home. But I'd be forever thankful that he was ours, if only for a day.

One-of-a-Kind Cat
Patty Darsnek

"Girlie must be the one cat you're not allergic to," my husband, Jim, said. It didn't make any sense. I'd agreed to keep a friend's cat for three weeks, knowing I was highly allergic.

I figured I'd just add allergy pills to my daily medical regimen, since I was already managing type 1 diabetes. But a week had passed and I hadn't taken one allergy pill. Even with Girlie curled up on our bed at night, none of my usual symptoms had shown up. "What is it about you?" I asked her one night when I climbed in bed.

Later I woke up to Jim's gentle shakes. "We have to check your blood sugar!" he was saying. The sheets were wet. I was covered in sweat. My blood sugar was dangerously low—life-threatening. Jim gave me a shot to raise it quickly. "I would have slept through the crisis if Girlie hadn't batted me in the face with her paws," Jim said.

Girlie never went back to my friend's house. She curls up with me every night, like a guardian angel watching over me. And, of course, no one is allergic to angels.

Sea of Angels

Juliette Anderson

PICHILEMU, MY CHILEAN HOME, is known as the "Capital of the Surf." People come from all over the world to ride our waves. My husband, Mitch, and I have lived here since the eldest of our five children was a baby, surfing and spreading the Gospel, living it in our home, as well.

A couple of Easters ago, I was focused especially on our youngest, thirteen-year-old Katrina. We'd been talking about Easter in preparation for the upcoming service, but I wasn't sure how much had really gotten through. Katrina has Down syndrome, and often had trouble making herself understood. How could I know my daughter's questions so I could fully convey the power of the Easter message?

"Why don't we go to the beach?" I said. Floating on our surfboards in God's ocean seemed a pretty good place to talk about miracles.

"Yay!" Katrina said, and ran off to find her powder-blue board. She was a strong swimmer on the local team and a good surfer too. That was no surprise in my family—Mitch would rather surf than eat, and I'd been a lifeguard for years in California. Katrina had a childlike wonder about the sea. Sand castles, surfing, starfish—it was all magical to her. Through her eyes it was magical to me too.

The beach was packed, and we threw our stuff down near some neighbors. Sun sparkled off the water. A few surf schools were having lessons in the shallow, peaceful bay. Beyond them, out in deeper waters, I could see waves of thirty feet or more. Only the most experienced surfers ventured out there. One of the kids in our group was a beginner, so, ever the lifeguard, I went with her down to the water and took my time settling her on her surfboard—too much time for Katrina. I let her paddle in ahead of us. "Not past those people," I told her, pointing to some surfing students. "I want to be able to see you."

"Okay, Mom!" she called, heading off in her shiny black wet suit.

The waters of the bay were shallow enough that if Katrina had any trouble, she could walk right out.

I turned back to see Katrina several yards away—and still paddling fast. "Katrina!" I shouted, surprised at her. "Come back!"

Katrina kept going, disappearing among the surfing students. "Katrina!" I took off after her. This was not the day for a game of chase.

It's not easy to go after someone on a surfboard. Lying flat against the water's surface, it's impossible to see anything. I paddled a few strokes, then sat up and scanned the water, squinting into the sunlight reflected off the ocean's spray. She couldn't have gotten very far. My arms were longer and I was stronger. Perhaps I'd passed her? I twisted around to look up at the cliffs behind me, where a couple was walking. "Hello!" I yelled up to them. "Can you see a girl on a blue surfboard out there?"

The couple scanned the water. Almost immediately the woman pointed to the north—way farther than I had believed Katrina could be. But sure enough, there she was, four hundred yards away, on the other side of a sand bar—beyond the bay and well into dangerous waters. I couldn't believe it.

"Katrina!" I screamed. People turned at the fear in my voice. All I could do was watch helplessly as Katrina rose up on a wave, crashed to the bottom, and disappeared.

"We'll find her!" a man called out. He and his friends headed toward her on their surfboards.

I twisted back to the couple on the cliff. "Please run to the surf shop!" I said. "My little girl's out there. We need the Coast Guard!"

The couple rushed off. Lifeguards splashed into the water; the surf instructors swam past me. People on the beach saw the commotion and moved to the water's edge. With swift, powerful strokes I paddled out of the bay into the waters beyond, to the last place I'd seen Katrina. Then I sat up and scanned the surf again. The sunlight reflecting off the mist on the water made it almost impossible to see anything. I looked at my watch. It had been thirty minutes since Katrina had left me. I swam back to shore and stumbled up to one of the lifeguards. "Did anyone find her?"

"Not so far," he said. "I'm only getting reports of a pod of *toninas*."

The Chilean dolphins were rarely seen around Pichilemu. These must have been migrating to warmer waters for mating season. Katrina had never seen one. Imagining how her face would have lit up at the idea of a pod of black dolphins, my throat closed up and my eyes filled with tears. *Lord, please send Your angels to help her.* I ran up and down the shore, squinting into the mist. Out in the water, the searchers did the best they could, but the big waves made it hard for them to get very far. Once more I paddled out on my board, hoping for a glimpse of Katrina. When I didn't find her I returned to the beach and scanned the children's faces there, hoping against hope Katrina would suddenly appear among them.

A friend from the surf shop came up beside me. "How long has she been missing?" he asked.

I looked at my watch. "Two hours!" I sobbed. It seemed like only minutes had passed since I'd watched her crash down from that wave.

"She's a strong swimmer," he reminded me. "Don't give up hope."

I couldn't give up hope. I bowed my head. I'd brought Katrina here today to teach her about miracles.

"I'm going to jog up the beach," I said. "Follow the current north." Off I went, but what did I expect to find? Katrina was in the water somewhere. There was little chance she'd get back to shore after all this time. Never had the promise and hope of Easter seemed so far away.

Another man jogged toward me from the other direction. "Have you seen a little girl with a blue surfboard?" I asked.

The man pointed north and jogged on by. Had he seen her? I shielded my eyes from the sun and looked into the distance.

There, on the beach ahead, was a little figure in a black wet suit. She was sitting on the shore building a sand castle. Beside her was a powder-blue surfboard. "Katrina!" She looked up.

"Mom!" She scrambled and ran into my arms. "Scary!" she said, pointing to the ocean. I asked her how on earth she made it back to shore.

"Dolphins, Mom!" said Katrina.

Dolphins? I didn't know Katrina had learned the word.

"Sticky noses!" said Katrina. She poked her own nose forward, imitating the creatures she described. Then she used her hands to show them leaping in and out of the water. She made sweeping gestures with her arms, as if she was swimming, and looked from side to side. Little by little I began to understand: Katrina was swimming and the *toninas* surrounded her, touching her with their wet noses until she grabbed on to the dorsal fin of one of the pod. Then she'd just let him pull her back to shore.

Everyone gave a great cheer when we got back to the beach. We called in the searchers. The guys from the surf shop had brought Mitch from home, and he swept Katrina into his arms. She told the whole crowd about her magical dolphin adventure. I'd brought Katrina to the beach to teach her about miracles, but I never dreamed we'd witness one firsthand. Never had the promise and hope of Easter seemed so near.

Tina

B. J. Taylor

"Look what I found," Dad said when he entered our small ranch house in a suburb of Phoenix. He cradled something in his arms, but we couldn't tell what it was.

A baby rabbit maybe? A cat? "What is it, Daddy?" I asked.

He moved one of his hands and a tiny brown face emerged. Then two ears sprung up along with a head barely the size of a small apple.

Dad knelt down and set the little sprite on the floor. Her long legs unfolded from his arms and we found ourselves staring at the tiniest dog we'd ever seen.

"She's so little."

"She's a Chihuahua. Probably a miniature," Dad reached out and petted her silky fur. "When I went around to lock up for the night I found her, abandoned in the ladies' room."

"Can we keep her?" I asked. Times were tough. Our move to Phoenix had been costly and Dad was trying to make his new gas station a success. We'd always had pets and missed our dogs and cats. We'd found them good homes before we moved, but the house . . . and our lives . . . weren't the same without them.

Dad looked at us. Three girls and one boy rounded out the family with our mother standing beside us. Mom was used to this. Dad had brought home many strays from the station he owned back in Wisconsin, but this was the first one here.

"Please, Daddy, please?"

"Okay, this one is so small"—Dad looked up at Mom—"she won't eat much."

We giggled with delight and stepped forward to pet the new addition to our home. Our little brother Peter, just two years old, toddled over and plopped down on the carpet next to her. The dog sniffed him, then snuggled up to his side.

"What should we name her?" Mom asked.

"Let's name her Tiny," my oldest sister said.

"How about Teeny?" chimed in my younger sister.

Mom stepped in and scooped her up with one hand. "Let's call you Tina."

And that's the name that stuck.

Tina brought a joyful noise back into our family. She made us laugh when she ran around the room, her huge ears perched upon her little head. Peter played with her endlessly and Tina loved it; they became an inseparable duo.

We lived in a mid-sized home on a street lined with palm trees. An idyllic yet modest setting. Surrounding us were many other homes the same size, with the majority holding swimming pools in the backyards. Mom was extremely concerned that Peter would fall in a neighbor's pool and drown, since he couldn't swim. Within a week of summer's arrival, we were at the local community center taking swimming lessons from a deeply tanned Hawaiian man with a booming voice.

Peter took to the instructor, and to the water, like a fish. He jumped in off the edge, not even holding his nose, and sank under the water. As his natural buoyancy floated him to the surface, he dog-paddled to the side.

"That a boy," the instructor said. He plucked him out of the water and hoisted him up to the edge of the pool. "Do it again."

With a wide, wet grin, Peter would smile, laugh, and jump in over and over again. It didn't take long before the instructor certified him as safe near pools.

Mom felt confident that if Peter was around one of the pools at a neighbor's house, he could swim if he fell in.

"Do you feel better now?" Dad asked her later.

"Much better," she replied.

That first summer went by in a flash. When school started in the fall, Tina pranced to the end of the driveway and saw all three of us girls off. Mom said that after Tina watched the bus leave she raced up the driveway and back into the house, leaping from her spindly legs into the waiting arms of my little brother, where she twitched her pointy ears and flashed her gorgeous big, brown eyes.

One night after dinner, I was off to visit a new friend who lived two streets over. "Bye, Mom, I'll be back before dark." I bounded out the screen door.

At the end of the driveway I looked both ways for cars then crossed to the other side. Heading down the block, I focused on the swaying palm trees and the feel of the sun as it kissed the hair on my arms and only slightly registered in my mind that a car headed down the street behind me.

"Barbie, Barbie, wait!"

My brother's cry pierced my thoughts and I turned around. There, half a block down the street, trailed my little brother. As he blindly ran out into the street, the car I'd heard gained ground and was now closer.

Time stood still. There was no way to reach my brother in time before he crossed the street right in front of the car's path. And from the speed of the car, I could tell the driver would never be able to stop in time.

That's when it happened. A blur, a streak, a squeal, and the sound of that car skidding to a stop. Tina was thrown to the side of the road.

Mom came running out of the house and scooped up my crying brother. Dad was right behind her. He gently lifted Tina into his arms and cradled her close to his body, just like he did that first day when he brought her home.

Within a matter of minutes, I was holding Tina in a blanket while Dad drove as fast as he could to the vet's. It was there we learned Tina didn't make it. The vet said her tiny body was no match for a tire on a massive car.

When I'd left the house that evening and heard the screen door bang against the frame, I didn't know it didn't latch. Peter was able to slip out without a sound.

Tina wasn't with us long—that crazy, squeaky, long-legged little wisp of a dog. Just long enough to accomplish God's plan for her: a fearless, angelic act of courage that saved my brother's life.

An Angel Dog Named Ginger
Pat Rogers

"SHOO, GINGER!"

I waved my hands at my neighbor's golden Lab. Ginger wagged her tail and gave another sharp bark.

"Your mom is probably wondering where you're at, buddy."

I pointed in the direction of Janet's condominium. The friendly dog gave me a long look before she lowered her ears and turned away.

Ginger's "mom," my neighbor Janet, was an active senior citizen. Yoga, art classes, and bus trips were common events for her. She often had a camera in her hands and I admired the way she always seemed to keep herself busy.

"Just got back from Branson!" she'd wave at me as she unloaded her suitcase. "You should see the shows they put on down there!"

Or, "Come over and I'll show you some photos from the St. Louis Zoo. I love the giraffes, don't you?"

But I hardly ever saw Ginger without Janet close by. Oh, Ginger got away now and then, but usually Janet was quick to follow.

A scraping at my back patio door alerted me once again to Ginger's presence. I stuck my head out and shivered.

"*Brrr,* Ginger." I patted her on the head. "You go home now. Janet shouldn't have to look for you in this cold. No treats today."

When was the last time I'd seen Janet? Had it been yesterday or the day before? Maybe even a few days before that. We'd spoken briefly as Ginger tugged on her leash.

"Ginger walks me," Janet had confessed with a laugh, pulling her coat tighter as the cold wind ruffled her hair. She coughed into her hand.

"Are you feeling okay?" I asked. "That cough doesn't sound too good."

"I'm fine. Just a cold." She stuck her hand back in her pocket. "Ginger is good company though. She barely leaves my side."

But Ginger had left her side today, I worried. Was my neighbor all right?

"*Woof! Woof!*"

Ginger again. Her brown eyes were anxious as she danced on my patio.

"Okay, girl. I'm coming."

Throwing on a sweater, I dashed to Janet's condo.

"Janet?" I called. I hesitated in the open doorway. "Ginger insists I come over. Are you all right?"

"In here," she whispered from the couch. "I knew Ginger would get help."

Janet's fragile appearance was enough to make me grab the phone and dial 911. As I hung up the phone, I was startled to see her get up from the couch.

"Janet, what are you doing?" I grasped her elbow as she struggled to reach her bedroom.

Her complexion turned ashen as she leaned against her dresser. With some effort, she tugged at a drawer and rummaged through her clothing. "I can't let anyone see me like this," Janet said. "I have to find something to wear."

But before she could select something, even before I could catch her, Janet's eyes rolled back in her head and she slipped to the floor.

"Janet!" I knelt down at her side. "Janet!" I listened to her raspy breathing as I felt her forehead. She was burning up. I stood up and grabbed a pillow to place under her feet.

Where is that ambulance? I wondered as Janet's eyelids fluttered, then closed again. *Why is it taking so long?* I wasn't sure what, if anything, I should do next.

Please, God, send help soon!

Ginger had been standing at the doorway, as if on guard, but now she whined low in her throat. A worried sound.

"Come here, girl," I said. "Your mom needs you."

Ginger needed no further urging. She lay down right beside Janet, her front paws protectively covering Janet's hand.

The keening of sirens had never sounded so good and I rushed to the door to wave at the oncoming ambulance.

"In here." I pointed down the hallway. "She's fainted and hasn't regained consciousness."

"Good thing you found her," an EMT informed me as they emerged from the bedroom a few minutes later. "She'll have to be hospitalized. Probably pneumonia."

On the gurney, Janet awoke and I reached for her hand. "You'll be all right now," I soothed.

"Please watch over Ginger for me," Janet said as she was loaded into the ambulance.

"I will," I assured her. "Ginger is your guardian angel. I'll take good care of her."

Janet nodded and her eyes closed once again before the back doors of the ambulance were slammed shut.

Between Janet's daughter and myself, Ginger was well taken care of, but she was one happy dog when her mom was released from the hospital. Ginger greeted me with a wagging tail and a happy, toothy grin when I walked over to welcome my neighbor back home.

Over a cup of coffee, Janet told me about her diagnosis and her stay at the hospital.

"I didn't understand how sick I was," she admitted. "That bronchitis got worse so quickly that I didn't even know I had pneumonia. I just thought I felt terrible and I'd get over it."

"Ginger knew though," I said, rubbing a soft, fluffy ear. "She was so adamant that day when she came to get me. She just wouldn't give up."

"Ginger even made it into my medical records," Janet announced proudly.

"What do you mean?"

"I told them about Ginger finding you. The doctor said if I'd gone much longer without medical treatment, the outcome might have been much, much worse. Ginger was the talk of the hospital."

"I'm so grateful she came to get me," I said. "Ginger saved your life."

"She certainly did," Janet agreed and tossed a snack in the air.

Ginger snapped the treat in midair and settled down with a satisfied sigh by Janet's chair.

Even if not visible to our eyes, Janet and I would be quick to agree that Ginger's wings are firmly attached to her broad, golden shoulders.

Out of the Storm

Emma Stenehjem

I DIDN'T EXPECT THE STORM to break until later that day. When the sky cracked open and the rains began, I was still driving on the main road with my granddaughter MaryBeth. The wind howled, swirling bits of sagebrush around my little car, and I peered anxiously out of the windshield. My farm in Arnegard was still twelve miles away! Then I remembered the shortcut around some grazing land.

It was a gravel road, deeply rutted by tractor marks, as is common in these rural parts of North Dakota. Something warned me not to risk it, but darkness was coming on and I was anxious to get home. I came to the fork and turned off the paved road.

"How did your practice go, MaryBeth?" I asked brightly. I knew my ten-year-old granddaughter was deathly afraid of storms. She had come to spend the Easter holiday with me and, to pass the time, had joined the church choir. Tomorrow, Easter Sunday, they would be singing the beautiful "Hallelujah Chorus" from Handel's *Messiah*.

"It was fine, Grandma," MaryBeth said in a small voice, keeping her eyes on the road.

I zigzagged along, grumbling each time I swerved to miss the giant cuts of the tractors. Then suddenly, as I rounded a curve, a blur of lights exploded in front of me. Horrified, I pulled hard on the wheel. A big car swooshed by, crowding us into a deep rut. The steering wheel jerked out of my hands and the car flipped over. We rolled over one more time into the roadside ditch. Then an eerie stillness filled the car except for the furious drumming of the rain . . .

Dazed, I tried to move myself. The crash had pushed me under the steering wheel and into the leg space in front of the driver's seat. I heard a weak whimper from the backseat. "Are you hurt, child?" I called.

There was a brief silence. Then a faint voice said, "I think I'm okay, Grandma."

I remembered stories I had heard of cars bursting into flames with the occupants trapped inside. "Come to me if you can," I called frantically. I knew I was too hurt to move to her. My legs were twisted and there was a strange heaviness in my chest.

The car had landed on its roof and MaryBeth had to crawl along it, pushing aside the seat cushions that had come loose and blocked her way. In a few moments I saw her frightened face peering at me from between the spokes of the steering wheel.

"Lord, forgive me for bringing this upon her," I groaned to myself. But there was no time to chide myself for choosing the shortcut. I had to think of a way to get help. Should I send my frightened granddaughter out in the rain where lightning flashes cracked across the sky? There was little chance of another car coming by and seeing us because we were hidden from the road. Dismally, I recalled that my husband wouldn't return from a business trip until tomorrow. The rest of my family wouldn't come by until it was time for tomorrow's church service. There was only one solution. MaryBeth would have to go out in the storm that terrified her and look for help.

My eyes searched the car for an opening. Just before the crash, MaryBeth had partially cranked down her steamed-up window to see out, and it was still open. "Crawl through the window, child," I told her feebly.

Soon she managed to wiggle out into the rain. "I'm scared, Grandma," she wailed through the wind and thunder crashes.

"Don't be frightened," I called. "Look for a light or a house." There was silence. Then at last she said. "I think I see some lights!"

"Go to them," I urged, and prayed for God to be with her as she splashed off through the fields.

I tried to free myself, but it was useless. The pain in my legs and chest was becoming unbearable, and I had to rest my head against the steering wheel for support. "Dear God, please protect and guide MaryBeth," I prayed over and over again. "Send Your guardian angel to be with her!"

The rain continued to pour on the crushed car as I waited and prayed. It seemed like hours and hours. What had happened to MaryBeth? Had she found someone? Was she lost in the storm?

Faith had always been strong in my family. We came to the farmlands three generations ago from Norway, and had always lived by the land and our faith. "My faith looks up to Thee, Thou Lamb of Calvary," I repeated to myself over and over.

I don't know how long I lay in the car, praying. But suddenly through the steady movement of the rain and wind I began to detect a new motion. What was it—a rubbing? Craning my neck painfully, I was able to see cows nudging my wrecked car!

"Hiyah, hiyah! Get home, you critters!" I heard someone shouting.

It's a farmer, I thought joyfully. I began to call for help.

"What's that?" came a startled reply from out in the storm. Soon a rain-soaked farmer was peering through the opened window of my car. I tried to smile at him. "Are you hurt?" he cried, vainly trying to pull open the jammed door.

"Somewhat," I answered weakly. "But I can't move and had to send a little girl for help. She's out there somewhere . . ." I looked helplessly into the fields.

"Don't worry," the man said. "We found her in my field. My cattle strayed in the storm and I found her right in the middle of my cows. She was so frightened and exhausted that she wasn't able to make any sense, so I brought her back to my house. Then I came on horseback to round up the cattle, and found you." He shook his head. "It's amazing. I wouldn't have seen a darn thing in this storm if it weren't for these here cows!"

Suddenly I knew how the Lord had answered my prayers. He'd sent the cows! They were our guardian angels—a herd of cows!

The farmer took off his horse's saddle blanket and covered me with it, promising to go for help. Soon I was taken to Arnegard Hospital. MaryBeth, already there, rushed to my side.

"You'll be all right now, Grandma," she said happily.

I nodded, thinking about God's special answer to my prayers. My old body would mend. MaryBeth was safe. She would still be able to sing that wonderful song of praise at Easter Mass.

"Yes, child," I said to her, "the 'Hallelujah Chorus' will surely be sung in church tomorrow!"

An Angel Named Bear

Dora Harris

WHAT ON EARTH? *That sounded like a gunshot!* I ran to look out the picture window in my front room, stumbling over my own feet as I went. The front door flew open and my twelve-year-old son, Shawn, hollered, "Mom, did you hear that noise? The car down the street backfired." I knew I should feel relieved, but my body trembled like a leaf in an Oklahoma twister. The changes in our neighborhood left me feeling on edge.

We'd lived in our close-knit middle-class community for years. Neighbors gossiped and knew everybody's business, but in times of need we could count on each other. Most of our neighbors owned their homes and had lived in the neighborhood for years. That changed as many of our friends moved out and more homes were turned into rental properties. I missed knowing my neighbors. I didn't know if a stranger walking down our street was a neighbor or someone up to no good.

One warm day in late March, Shawn and I spent the afternoon taking advantage of the nice weather to take care of outdoor chores. The muscles between my neck and shoulders ached as we put away our tools. Our new neighbor called out, "Did you hear about the robbery down the street?" My muscles tensed more, this time from a sense of apprehension.

We chatted for a few minutes before I finished our cleanup. Out of nowhere a big furry dog lumbered into our yard and greeted us like a returning soldier greets his family. "Shawn, come look at this big ol' dog. He looks like a bear," I hollered.

The dog's tail thumped with excitement as Shawn appeared around the corner. Shawn managed to keep his balance as the dog tackled him and slathered his face with dog hugs and kisses. It seemed strange because the dog acted as though he knew us well.

"Let's show Gary!" My twenty-seven-year-old son worked nights and needed to wake up. As I headed back inside, the dog bounded into the house. I couldn't stop him!

Laughing, I shouted to Gary, "Come see what we found." The moment the dog saw Gary, he jumped up on him, greeting him as a long-lost friend. "Where did he come from?" Gary asked as he wiped dog slobbers from his face.

We dug through the fur and found a collar and a tag. The tag described the dog as a German shepherd. We called the veterinarian's number listed on the tag. The receptionist checked the vet's records and confirmed that the dog was a German shepherd. *That's odd*, I thought as I looked down at the St. Bernard lying on the carpet in front of me. The receptionist gave me a phone number for the owner, which I called. The phone had been disconnected.

My husband, Ansel, thought we should continue trying to locate the dog's owners. I knew the loss of beloved pets in the past made him wary of becoming attached. Over the course of the next few weeks we checked the newspapers and bulletin boards of nearby businesses for ads of missing dogs. A couple of the ads fit the description but turned out to be the wrong dog. The dog's affectionate behavior caused us to believe he belonged to a family, and we wanted to reunite him with them. In the meantime, we named him Bear.

Reports of another burglary at the house behind us stirred up a sense of impending danger unlike anything I'd experienced before. I went to bed hoping for needed rest.

That night I tossed and turned in sleep, unable to pull myself from the tangled web of a nightmare. *I crept through the dark room hoping the noise coming from the front door of my home stemmed from my overactive imagination. Creak! I hesitated. I strained to hear—nothing. With greater confidence I moved toward the window and peered out. Someone stood outside the door. My throat caught.* Run! *I told myself. But my body refused to move. I reached out and felt thick fur as a scary-looking intruder burst through the front door. I heard a deep-throated growl from a dog beside me. The stranger turned and ran.*

I awakened in a cold sweat. Ansel tried to comfort me as I told him about the dream. Then I realized the dog in the dream was Bear! *Had God sent Bear to protect us?* Ansel took the dream as a warning and said, "That dog isn't going anywhere!" We stopped searching for Bear's previous owner.

In the past Ansel always objected to pets coming into the house, but Bear wielded special favor. Ansel and the kids delighted in coaxing Bear to get me to bake cinnamon rolls. Bear loved the sweet treats. When someone mentioned, "cinnamon rolls," Bear set to work persuading me to go bake the rolls by putting his head under my arms, nudging me out of my chair and into the kitchen. He ate his fair share when they came out of the oven.

Over the next four months, Bear became a part of the family. We enjoyed Bear's company and I felt safer with him around. That summer we celebrated the Fourth of July weekend on the Illinois River. A neighbor took care of Bear during our brief absence. Gary went home a day before the rest of the family. I didn't know which he missed more, his girlfriend or Bear.

When we arrived home, Gary was upset. "I opened the front door of our house and before I knew what was happening Bear shot through the doorway like a bullet and disappeared. A bunch of our neighbors helped me look for him. He's nowhere to be found."

Around the same time of Bear's departure, the police arrested a group of men for the burglaries in our neighborhood. Despite the empty place in our hearts, we believed that God sent our angel named Bear on assignment to another family. Although we no longer needed Bear's protection, we will always miss his companionship.

CHAPTER 4

Mysterious Messengers

"Last night an angel of the God to whom I belong and whom I serve stood beside me."

—Acts 27:23 (NIV)

Angels in the Mississippi Mud

Marci Seither

THE VAN PICKED US UP at the airport and drove through the desolate neighborhood. Cars, now useless, were strewn around on quiet streets. Homes, lined in neat rows, were dark.

"Welcome to New Orleans," said the driver. A bedspread tangled in the branches of a tree flapped in the wind, waving an eerie greeting.

It had been five months since Katrina pounded the coast. The horrifying images we had seen on television from the comfort of our California homes didn't compare to what we tried to comprehend in the ravaged part of our country that looked like a war zone.

"It looks like King Kong and Godzilla were fighting," said Jack, who was five at the time. I nodded and squeezed his hand.

When my husband, John, had first suggested our whole family go on a disaster relief team, I was apprehensive about taking our five kids. Eventually I agreed that helping others would be a good experience. Now, as we drove toward Bay Saint Louis, Mississippi, I wondered if it was a mistake.

The group of twenty-seven volunteers we traveled with pulled into the parking lot of an old school, now converted to the Emergency Operations and FEMA headquarters. Amid crates of bedding, boxed kitchen sets, and other needed supplies, we assembled our cots, unrolled our sleeping bags, and unpacked our work clothes. For the next six days this was home.

John and our older two kids worked on construction projects and at the mill. I was on the team that helped at an abandoned-gym-turned-warehouse, where trucks delivering disaster relief aid could be sorted and stored. We were three miles from the bay, yet the nine-foot water mark on the cold gray cement brick walls was a grim reminder of the far-reaching effects of the hurricane. I worked with our three youngest children and Bob, an elderly volunteer from Nebraska. Bob drove the forklift while the kids and I sorted canned food and other supplies.

"Hello . . . hello?" came a voice that startled me. A ragged-looking stranger sauntered into the gymnasium, his hair snarled and unwashed. It was much more than his disheveled outward appearance that bothered me. After all, I had worn the same work clothes for several days, as well. I couldn't put my finger on it, but something wasn't right. My stomach tightened. He looked around at the pallets of food and basic household necessities lining the cold cement walls then grinned, as if pleased with his discovery.

"This is really cool." He made a sweeping gesture with his hand. "We had no idea you had this here and it's exactly what we need. Maybe we can work together."

He introduced himself as Ray and mentioned that his organization's portable kitchen had recently been shut down by county health officials. Now, they were looking for a new food source and a place to reestablish their camp.

Through the open gym door I could see a few others who had come with him drift in and out of sight. I tried to keep my mind on my task and my eyes on our kids. *It's just someone who wants to help.* I tried to shake off the uneasiness, but my stomach tightened even further. I quickly made a mental evaluation of our situation. I didn't have a phone. We had been dropped off and didn't have a car. The able-bodied men from our group were all at different sites. We were far from home. I tried to shake anxiety off but it stuck with me as tight as the Mississippi mud that now clung to my boots. I came to help others. Now I couldn't even help myself—let alone protect my own children.

Jack alerted me that he urgently needed to use the portable restroom. We quickly excused ourselves to the outhouses situated at the edge of the parking lot.

I kept my eye on the open gym door. Every once in a while I saw a glimpse of Ray talking with Bob. The other three or four people who had arrived with Ray now meandered around the littered playground before disappearing into the building's shadows.

I forced myself to breathe. My other children, Scott and Amy, were still inside and it felt like Jack was taking forever. I saw another person linger at the entrance of the doorway. Thoughts of the unspeakable began to play out in my imagination. "C'mon, Jack. Mom needs you to be a little quicker." *God, I don't feel good about this*, I prayed. *You are going to have to do something here. And please hurry!*

The sound of gravel crunching beneath tires diverted my attention. A brown sedan pulled to a stop in front of the vacant school building. Through the open car windows I saw four men. They were clean shaven and dressed in casual button-up shirts. Fighting my apprehension to ask complete strangers for help, I took a dozen steps toward their car.

"Where are you from?" I put my hands deep in my overall pockets, hiding the fact they had begun to shake.

The driver leaned forward, looked me in the eye, and asked, "What do you need?"

His question surprised me. Looking around at the situation and conditions we were in, wouldn't it have been easier to ask, what *don't* you need?

"Men." My bold answer surprised me.

I summed up the situation, the surprise visitors, and my uneasiness. They got out of the car and followed me and Jack, now at my side, toward the gymnasium. Ray, his back to the door, was still talking to Bob. Without saying another word, the four men walked in and positioned themselves between Ray and the back of the warehouse, where my other two children were still sorting out canned goods. The men didn't utter a word. All four had the same solid build, but what really captured my attention was how clean they were, especially compared to those of us who had been in Mississippi helping.

As if aware of their presence, Ray turned around. "Well, we had better go now."

The four men continued quietly standing there until Ray's car sputtered to life, rattled out of the parking lot, and disappeared down the street.

"Thank you so much," I said, shaking each man's hand. "You are an answer to my prayer."

The driver of the car smiled. "Maybe we're your angels."

That night the group gathered after our cafeteria-style dinner to talk about the day. I shared how God's provision for us that day didn't come on a pallet or box. It came in an older model sedan driven by angels who heard a mother's anxious prayer for help.

Only Human?

Arlene Beilage

Should I chance it? The puddle blocking the entrance of the doctor's office parking lot had to be at least a foot deep. It practically made waves. The cars in front of me didn't share my hesitation; they drove straight through. I pressed down on the gas and followed.

The engine died. The dashboard lit up. My car wouldn't budge.

Sudden tropical downpours are a danger in South Florida, especially for someone in their seventies. The whole drive here, I could scarcely see more than a few feet in front of me through the rain. Now, half of my car stuck out into the street. Cars swerved around me to avoid a collision. *What do I do?*

I took out the key, opened the door, and stepped into the water—almost up to my knee. As soon as I did, an odd-looking pickup truck pulled over.

It seemed from another era. The truck bed was made from wooden slats. A short, scruffy man emerged. "I'm here to help you," he said.

He waded into the water beside me. "Get back into your car," he said. "It will start now. Drive on and park."

I don't know why, but I believed him. I climbed back in my car, stuck the key in the ignition, and turned it. The engine roared! I forded through the puddle and parked in a spot right by the front door. Rushing inside, I realized I'd forgotten to thank the man. I turned around, but he must have driven on.

I called my husband and told him what happened. "I'll come by, just in case the car won't start again," he said. But the engine did start, no problem. Like it had never been flooded at all.

The Far Side of Midnight

Irene Kutz

FROM THE TIME I WAS A CHILD my parents taught me to believe in God and to know Him. But as I grew up I learned that knowing God and being a professed Christian does not always keep difficulties or heartbreak away. Indeed, there was one time in my life when I felt that God had deserted me altogether.

It happened during World War II, when I was only twenty. Allen was twenty-one. He was in the artillery, the Timberwolf division. He was a Christian, too, and we pledged our lives together and our love to God.

When Allen went overseas with his division, a part of him stayed with me. We were to be married when he returned. We prayed for an early end to the war.

But then there was the Battle of the Bulge. Allen did not come through it.

Words cannot express the agony I felt. From the beginning, from the first time we met, our lives had been so intertwined I had felt that there could be no life for me if his ceased. I could not see how a loving God could permit such sorrow to come to me.

The night I learned of Allen's death was one of heavy, gloomy rain. Unable to talk to anyone, I put on my slicker and hat, and went out to walk in the downpour, trying to escape the unbearable loss, the despair. But they stayed with me.

I don't know how long I walked, or where I went, but finally I found myself on the bridge over the river that flowed through our town, an old-fashioned draw-bridge with a bridge-tender who stayed in a little house on the main span, raising the center section when boats came by. I knew he was there, but I was sure that he would not be able to see me in the darkness and the rain.

I leaned over the railing and gazed down into the churning water below, just barely visible by the lights of the town. I had always lived for God, trying to do His will, and now He had betrayed me. If I could just slip over the side into the dark water, oh, the blissful oblivion, the release from pain. The agony of drown-ing would be over in moments—nothing compared to the torment now tearing me apart. *Oh, Allen,* I thought. *Allen, Allen . . .*

I heard no sound, but suddenly I felt a hand on my arm. "Come in out of the rain," the bridge-tender said quietly. Numbly I let him lead me to his tiny house on the bridge. He sat me down on one of the two chairs and poured a cup of cof-fee from his Thermos. Pain possessed me, consumed me. I felt as if I were pain.

"It's a nasty night to be out," he remarked. He had removed his slicker, and I did not recognize him as one of the regular men. He was a little man, with an ageless face, and his eyes—the bluest, deepest-set I had ever seen—were compas-sionate and kind. I had never seen him before, but I felt his spirit touching mine.

I began to cry, and he sat there, across the little table from me, saying noth-ing. Oddly, his silence didn't seem strange to me; he did not seem like a stranger.

A boat's whistle hooted three times down the river. The man set in motion the huge mechanism that raised the bridge. The boat passed through, and the bridge settled back into place.

My sobbing had quieted, and I found myself telling him about Allen, spilling out my soul as if I'd known him all my life. When I had finished, I felt drained, exhausted, but the unbearable knife-edge sharpness was gone.

His eyes stayed on my face as he said quietly, "I can understand your grief." Then he took both my hands in his. "Father," he murmured, "come to Your child."

He bowed his head in silent prayer for several minutes. Then he raised it. "Come now. I'll walk with you to the end of the bridge. The Lord will see you through this. Remember that."

I walked home. I still grieved, but the awful despair was alleviated. I knew somehow that God had not forsaken me. I felt I was no longer alone.

Several days later, I walked down to the river to tell the bridge-tender that I was slowly learning to live with my loss, and to thank him. But he wasn't there.

I described him to the man on duty.

"I don't know who you're talking about, miss, and I know all the tenders," he told me.

"But the night it rained so hard . . . ," I persisted.

"I'm sorry. I don't know who was on duty that night."

I never found out who that man was, and I know I never will.

But I do know Who sent him to me.

Penniless in Bangkok
Scott Springfield Domeij

THE PAUPER CLUTCHED a pulverized tin cup on his battered wheelchair's armrest. He resembled a stone Buddha perched stoically on his wheeled throne. Instead of knees, two stumps jutted out a few inches past his well-worn seat. Healed balls of skin capped his amputated stubs.

Each day for five days, I passed this beggar, who was surrounded by chaos. His back wheels were parked too near the curb's ledge, a hair's breadth from speeding cars almost shaving the back of his dilapidated wheelchair.

The sky train overhead sliced through the heat and humidity. Harried pedestrians swerved between the crowds packing the sidewalk, scrawny stray dogs, and speeding motorcycles that had jumped the curbs to escape traffic gridlock. A bouquet of garlic, ginger, and oil drifted from food carts. Trinket hawkers squawked at tourists.

Loose tiles, broken pavement, and sinkholes threatened to turn my ankles. How this disabled man navigated his wheelchair over cracks and gaping holes through the motorized and human congestion mystified me.

He was camouflaged by the urban landscape, and indifferent passersby hardly glanced at the beggar. I smiled, attempting to catch his eye. He focused straight ahead with a cold, blank stare.

I was on a tight budget, but I resolved to save all my loose coins to plunk in his cup before I left Thailand. Each time I ate a meal or shopped, I paid with only paper *baht*, the Thailand currency. My excitement rose as all of the change earmarked for the amputee weighed down my purse.

The morning of December 22, my last day in Bangkok, I caught the skytrain to the beggar's spot. My change clanked into his metal cup.

That's probably more money than he receives in a month.

His frigid eyes never blinked acknowledgment. Not one facial muscle communicated "thank you." *How many times had I taken God or others for granted when they provided small miracles?*

I made a few more impulsive purchases and received more change. I saw the paraplegic teetered on the filthy curb's edge between the busy street and crowded sidewalk. He seemed alive only from the waist up, since his shriveled legs looked as lifeless as his ancient, soiled wooden crutches. I burrowed deep into my purse, and my fingers scraped together more change. As the coins clinked into his cup, our gaze locked—two people from different worlds. His toothless smile and joyful eyes sparkled with thanks.

After returning to the hotel, I bargained hard with the taxi driver to avoid being overcharged for the ride to Bangkok International Airport. We agreed on a three hundred *bhat* fee. As we sped along the freeway, he said, "I miss my daughter. She live five hours away. To make money, I buy taxi and work in Bangkok. The cost of gas hurt my business."

From the debris littering his front seat, I suspected he ate and slept in his taxi. As a single mother, too often in the past I had worried I wouldn't have enough money to fill my tank with gas to drive to work.

At the Bangkok International Airport, the taxi driver unloaded and stacked my slippery plastic luggage onto a baggage cart. I pressed all my currency into his hand—five hundred baht (about $16.50), plus eight American dollars. I was flat broke, but I didn't need any money until I returned home. The taxi driver's beaming smile made my heart dance.

I dragged the unwieldy cart through the doors of the international departure building to my first checkpoint, the VAT (tourist value-added tax) desk.

The revenue officer stamped my VAT refund application. My boss had warned me that I had to pay an immigration exit tax before leaving Thailand, and I counted on the 1,400 baht ($46) VAT refund to pay that exit tax.

I waited for my cash refund only to be informed, "This is not the VAT refund counter." A slight spike of anxiety radiated from my chest to my throat.

After passing through security, I checked into China Airlines and received my boarding pass. The beautiful employee directed me toward the exit immigration tax window.

"I need my 1,400 baht VAT refund to pay my five hundred baht exit tax," I explained.

"The VAT refund office is in the departure lounge," the woman said. "You cannot pass through immigration without paying."

Despite my protests, she shook her head, waved me on, and turned to the next person in line.

An electrical current of panic streaked through my brain. I was stranded in Bangkok, five thousand miles from home, because I couldn't get to the departure lounge. I had no money.

Not one cent.

God, please don't let me miss my plane. It's Christmas. I want to get home to my family. Please, please, Lord, show me what to do.

Light-headed and weak-kneed, I wobbled to a bank kiosk.

"Can you charge five hundred baht to my credit card and give me cash?"

"We only exchange currency. Why don't you try the ATM over there?"

Panicky sweat rolled down my face. I slipped my credit card into the ATM, but I couldn't figure out how to use the "automatic" teller machine. Through blurry eyes, I spotted the squarish Thai lettering.

Instructions, I suppose. Great. I don't read Thai. I need help and I don't know one person in Bangkok who can help me.

I proceeded to the tourist information desk and poured out my story. "I need five hundred baht for the exit tax. I have a 1,400 baht VAT refund due on the other side of immigration. Can you *please* help me?"

The assistants smiled, shrugged their shoulders, and pointed me back to China Airlines.

How will I get home? I wish my boss had explained that the VAT refund office was located after *exiting immigration.*

Tears streamed down my face. I returned to China Airlines to ask for help. The airline employee who took my ticket was checking in another passenger with distinct Thai features—large round eyes, rounded nose, full lips, and sculpted cheekbones.

She seems unusually tall for a Thai—at least six feet tall, maybe taller.

Most Thais stand five-foot-four.

Distraught, I explained my Catch-22 predicament to the attendant. "If you can just let me go through to the departure lounge, I'll get the money and—"

"Traveling is stressful," the tall Thai woman said in a perfect American accent. "Here, take this."

I stared at the money she thrust into my palm. She had given me one thousand baht, more than enough.

"Thank you. I'll pay you back on the other side of immigration."

"Don't worry about it."

"What's your name?"

"Angela."

I dashed to immigration and slid five hundred baht under the immigration window and was cleared to go into the departure line. Waves of relief and joy refreshed my body as I prayed.

At last, I'm headed home. Wahoo! Thank You, God, for hearing my prayer and providing for me. Now I can get home to celebrate Your Son's birth with my two sons.

At the next turnstile, the immigration officer inspected my passport. "You overstayed your visa. That will cost an extra two hundred baht ($54) per day."

She allowed me to collect my refund from the VAT refund office, which paid the remaining overstay fees.

I entered the departure area and looked for Angela.

How did she slip through immigration without my seeing her?

I searched every China Airlines waiting lounge—no Angela. I looked carefully. Twice. I even checked the restrooms.

I decided she must already be on the plane, so I boarded my flight home. After takeoff, I walked up and down the two aisles from one end of the plane to the other and looked at every face.

No Angela.

I sat and pondered what had happened that day. I had given freely to those who had no way to repay—just as Jesus taught me to love my neighbor. The tall Thai woman had given just as freely to me, and I couldn't find the stranger to repay her.

Could Angela be an angel? Nah! Couldn't be. But how else can I explain . . . ?

Cold chills rippled up and down my body—and not from the plane's air-conditioning.

No Longer Abandoned

Judy Hampton

"THE CHURCH IS HOSTING a marriage enrichment seminar next month. It's only a day and a half long. Would you like to go?" I asked my husband, Orvy, timidly, knowing he'd probably pass on it.

"Sure!" he exclaimed.

I was shocked. Only two years had passed since we'd been in the middle of a total marriage meltdown. Divorce had seemed imminent.

Actually, life had been tough from the day we married.

I'd met my football-hero husband in high school. It was love at first sight. We married shortly after graduation, which was not that unusual for our era. Plus, I was pregnant.

Orvy went to college on a football scholarship, and I gave up college to work as a secretary and support our goal: his college degree. At night we juggled four part-time jobs.

Our life was hard, with periods of intense misery. We barely made ends meet and often went hungry. We had to save money to pay for the doctor and the hospital for when our baby was born.

Several months after our dismal wedding, our son entered the world. It was instant love, but this new responsibility added more financial burden, which stretched our patience and bank account to the breaking point.

With each year our marriage declined until I wanted to be anywhere but home. Our only hope was Orvy's getting out of college with a degree so we could capture the American dream. But right before his graduation, my world fell apart. I came home after work and found a letter propped up on the kitchen table: "Judy, I have to get away and find myself. I don't know what I want to do with my life since I didn't receive a pro football contract. I'm sorry."

I slumped into a chair. I'd been abandoned . . . *again*. Two days later I found out I was pregnant *again*.

Abandonment had actually been a backdrop for my whole life. From an early age I was worried sick because Daddy was always out of work. I didn't understand that his unemployment was because of his alcohol problem. Mom hid his problems, just as she hid her own alcohol abuse.

I was trained from a very young age to enable and feel sorry for my parents. I lived in a lot of fear because I knew they were not interested in physically taking care of me.

I felt emotionally abandoned, as well. Even though I was popular in high school—a cheerleader, in the royal court, a student leader—my parents never came to any events to support me or even cared what I did.

Fear became my constant companion: fear of poverty, and fear of failure. When I learned I was pregnant two months after high school graduation, I had another reason to be paralyzed with fear.

When I finally told my parents, they basically abandoned me *again*. They said I was a disgrace to our family. "You've made your bed, now sleep in it. You'll get no help from us."

True to their word, they never did help me. I fell into a deep depression and I wanted to run away, but I had no place to go. I gave up all my dreams of college and got married.

When my husband left me four years later, I realized I could never trust another soul.

A few weeks before our beautiful daughter's birth, my husband begged for forgiveness. He promised he'd spend the rest of his life making up for what he had put me through. Not only did I not believe him, I had little hope of our marriage surviving. But I was desperate so we reconciled.

Orvy got a job that paid well, and we moved into a bigger apartment. We tried desperately to put back the pieces of our shattered life, but each day fresh fear invaded my soul. I was consumed by thoughts of being abandoned again.

We tried to make our marriage work, but we lacked the power within for any long-term change. After two years of striving, something happened. I got a phone call from a friend who'd stood by me through thick and thin.

"Judy, are you going to be home this afternoon? I'd love to come by and see the kids," Harriet said. I assured her I would be home.

After we exchanged pleasantries, Harriet and I sat down for a cup of coffee, and she asked if she could share something with me. "Sure," I replied.

Harriet pulled out a small Gospel tract called "The Four Spiritual Laws." She began to read the first page. I was overwhelmed at the question, "Do you know that God loves you and has a plan for your life?"

I immediately started to cry. I didn't know whether God loved me or had abandoned me, as well. When Harriet got to the final pages of that tract, I was sobbing. She sweetly asked, "Judy, would you like to pray and receive Christ as your Savior?"

I nodded yes as tears streamed down my cheeks.

Right there in my tiny dining room, while the fall leaves were changing colors outside, Jesus was changing my heart.

A few hours later Orvy came home from work. He took one look at me and asked, "What's going on? What's happened? You look different."

I told him I'd become a Christian.

"Oh," he said matter-of-factly, "I did that when I was twelve!"

You sure could've fooled me, buddy, I thought, but I said nothing. I knew my life had been changed in a moment.

A few weeks later my husband had an encounter with Jesus Christ and recommitted his life to the Lord. God began to resurrect our dead marriage and set it on higher ground.

Three months after our life change, Orvy was transferred to Texas. There, someone from his office invited us to church.

We told no one about our painful past. We thought people would judge us for having had so many marital problems and having to get married. So we acted as though we were the cookie-cutter Christian family. A few months later we heard about the marriage enrichment seminar.

We arrived at the church on a Friday evening. Everyone was friendly and seemed to have their lives together much more than we did. But as the evening wore on we were astounded by the number of couples who openly talked about their marital problems and how Jesus Christ had changed them. We looked at each other as if to say, "I thought we were the only people in the free world with problems."

The day passed at warp speed.

"As we close this seminar, we would like to encourage you to go into the sanctuary, one couple at a time, and pray together," the leader instructed. We'd never prayed together in our entire married life.

We headed toward the sanctuary, a bit embarrassed about our prayer-less life. As we sheepishly stepped into the sanctuary, it was empty. A soft light from behind a large wooden cross illuminated the room. At the altar we held hands and awkwardly knelt to pray.

Before we could utter a word, someone came up behind us and nuzzled between us. He put his arms around us and began to pray.

Who is this guy? I wondered.

This stranger began to pray about things we'd never told a soul: our shameful past, our difficult marriage, and the years of strife, lost dreams, and separation.

He asked God to heal our marriage and encouraged us to seek Him with all our hearts and trust Him to provide all our needs. He prayed that we would put the past behind us and give our future to God.

His voice was so soothing, his words wrapped in so much love. I desperately wanted to turn around and get a glimpse of him, but I was too mesmerized by his presence. Tears flowed down my cheeks, tears of joy I'd never known in my life.

When he was finished, we stood and turned to thank this precious man, but no one was there. We were all alone in the dimly lit sanctuary.

It took some time before we comprehended what had taken place that day. We'd had a visit from an angel of the Lord. To this day we joyfully recall our time with our unexpected visitor.

This year we celebrate fifty-two years of marriage.

Our Snow Angel

Jill Kemerer

JANUARY BROUGHT BUCKETS OF SNOW, slick roads, and school cancellations galore. By day seven, I figured it was safe to treat our kids to lunch at a restaurant. We piled into our car and began the five-mile trip to Panera Bread.

My daughter had recently taken driver's training, and her gaze darted from me to the mini-mountains of snow lining the road. "Are you sure it's safe to drive?"

"Of course, I'll take it slow." I approached the on-ramp to the highway. "See? We're not the only ones out. The roads must be okay for traffic to be moving as quickly as it is."

As I prepared to merge onto the highway, I glimpsed a semitruck in the right lane. It showed no signs of slowing to let me enter. I had a dilemma—either apply the brakes and increase my chance of hitting the massive truck or accelerate to merge ahead of it. I chose to speed up.

My tires snagged a patch of thick slush, and our car pitched forward. As if in slow motion, we turned a complete circle in front of the semi and kept spinning. I watched in horror as another semitruck plunged straight toward the driver's side of my car. My son sat directly behind me. My daughter next to me. We were all a split second away from a terrible accident.

Instead of crashing, our car plunged into a huge snow drift in the median. The semi zoomed past!

Adrenaline surged through my veins, and every part of my body shook.

"Are you okay?" I asked my frightened kids. They assured me they were. We sat in silence a few minutes. My brain churned. How had that semi missed us? We were *right there*. It seemed impossible.

"It's a miracle," I said. After my nerves had calmed a bit, I said a silent thank-You prayer and put the car in reverse, but the tires failed to grip the ground beneath them. I tried pulling forward. Nope. We were stuck. Heavy traffic continued to pass us, but no one stopped to help. I called my husband and briefly explained the situation, assuring him we were fine but trapped.

A small, navy-blue Nissan approached, and a man in his twenties walked toward us. I told the kids to wait in the car as I enthusiastically greeted him. He reminded me of one of my hardworking cousins—capable, solid, and kind.

"I have a tow strap in my trunk." He inspected the angle my car rested. "Want me to try to pull you out?"

"Yes, please!"

"Be right back." He headed to his trunk. "Same thing happened to me last week so I keep the strap in here all the time. Never know when you might need it."

I shivered, rubbing my gloved hands together as the wind blew my hair around. The temperature was five degrees and the wind chill made it feel colder. I gestured to him. "What should I do?"

"Let me find a spot to hook this on." He bent to check the back bumper. Thick, wet snow covered the pavement.

"You'll get all wet and dirty." Poor man was obviously on his way somewhere. Last thing he needed was wet, freezing clothes. "Show me where it goes, and I'll do it."

"I'll take care of it." Crouching down, he eased his back onto the ground and fiddled under the bumper. Guilt and cold had me shifting from one foot to the next. How could I let this stranger plop down on the ice for me? And why, after fifteen minutes of being stuck, did this guy stop when no one else had?

His flushed face peeked out from under the trunk. "Almost got it. I'll attach it to my car and we'll try to pull you out." He stood, brushing the snow off his jeans.

"I can't thank you enough. I'm sorry your clothes are sopped."

"Don't worry about it. Get back in your car and when you feel a tug, put it in reverse. Then press the gas."

"Okay."

The car lurched as the strap engaged. Shifting in reverse, I pressed the gas.

Whirr. Sputter. Whirr. Clunk. Vrewww.

We barely moved. I floored it. Finally, the wheels gained traction. We were on the pavement again.

I raced outside, and thanked the man over and over. A question pressed on my heart.

"What's your name?" I asked.

A funny expression flashed in his eyes. "Michael."

Michael? Like the angel? My eyes widened. I'd uttered the words, *It's a miracle,* a mere half an hour ago. Could he be an angel? Only God could have nudged our car out of the way in time to avoid the accident, and only God would send someone in single-digit temperatures to rescue us.

"Please let me give you some money for helping me—"

He held up his palm. "No. I don't want anything."

I gave him a quick hug. "Thank you. And God bless you."

He smiled and walked away.

The man in the slouchy jeans might not have looked like one, but I know Michael was an angel sent to rescue us. And I'll always be grateful.

The Angel in the Flannel Shirt

Jeannine Rodriguez-Everard

As I was flying into Denver International Airport after being away for Christmas, I realized I had no idea where I'd parked my car. I had pulled into one of those long-term lots, which are huge in Denver—absolutely *huge*. So as the plane was landing, I was praying, "God, could You just remind me where I parked?"

But I was getting nothing.

When I boarded the shuttle bus for long-term parking, a guy sat down in front of me. He was wearing a flannel shirt and jeans. And he turned around right away and looked at me—and winked! It wasn't a flirtatious wink; it was more like he was telling me, "I know something you don't know." But then he got into a conversation with someone else, and I saw a friend of mine on the bus and started talking too. But as I was talking with my friend, I could overhear his conversation in front of me. He was saying that he'd been in Michigan for a couple of weeks.

As we approached the long-term lot, I still had absolutely no clue where my car was. So I decided I would get off at the first stop and just walk around and see what happened. Maybe I'd have to keep getting on and off the bus—just keep riding it until I found my car.

When I got off at the first stop, the guy in the flannel shirt got off at the same time. Now, I've just come home after being away for Christmas, and I am loaded down with bags, gifts, and all kinds of stuff—loads of stuff—and right away the guy said to me, "Are you looking for your car?"

"Yeah," I answered, "but I have absolutely no idea where I parked it."

"Well," he said, "my car is parked right over here. Why don't I give you a lift, and we'll just go find your car?"

Now, I would never normally get into a car with a stranger. But I just had this feeling that I could trust him. So he put my bags in the trunk, we got in, and immediately he said, "You know what? I have a sense your car is over in this other area of the parking lot."

Sure enough, he drove me right to my car. He got out, pulled all my luggage out, and put it into my car. It was just so easy—he simply drove to the other part of the garage, and there was my car.

When all my stuff was in my car, I asked, "What's your name?"

"Oh, my name is Brad."

"Oh, I'm Jeannine. Thank you so much. I can't even thank you enough."

As I got into my car, he drove away—and I just sat there and began thinking back over all the details. He said he'd been in Michigan for two weeks over Christmas, but he had no coat. He was wearing only jeans and a flannel shirt. He had no luggage with him, even though he said he'd been away for two weeks. His car was parked right at the shuttle-bus stop, and it was unlocked. He drove me directly to my car—like, *straight* to my car. On the bus he'd sat down right in front of me, turned around, and winked—which is when I realized the very last thing he did before saying good-bye, after he put my bags in my car and I thanked him, was give me that wink again!

I knew in that moment he was an angel!

But—and this is what amazed me and touched me the most. Even though I had always thought my first angelic encounter would be a major event with blinding, flashing white lights and some extreme message from God, it was a moment of personal need when the Lord showed His concern for me. It was cold, dark, and late that night flying into Denver, and the long-term parking lot was huge, and I didn't know where I'd parked my car. God sent an *angel* to help me out.

"There Is No Kay"
Sissy Burggraf

A COLD WINTER'S DAY THAT would change my life forever. Leaving the unheated horse barn, I began unzipping my outer coveralls to start the removal of my five layers of clothes as I did every day after caring for my rescued horses. Remembering I had to go to an out-of-town garage to pick up a Christmas present for my husband, I decided to leave my heavy layer alone and go as I was; after all, there would only be a bunch of guys there who would care less what I looked like and I was short on time!

A few hours later, about eight miles from home, found me traveling along Stoutsville Pike in my little Chevy S-10 pickup truck, nearing the intersection of Sixteenth Road; an intersection in Pickaway County, Ohio, well-known for its many fatalities, the latest being only a couple of weeks earlier.

The area is flat and open in all directions so even though I had the right-of-way on the fifty-five-mile-per-hour stretch of road, I slowed down to forty-five miles per hour, scanning the road both ways to be sure there wasn't any traffic that might fail to stop for the stop signs. *NOTHING* either direction but as I entered the intersection, something caught my eye. I turned my head to look just as the full-size Ford F150 came blasting into the intersection!

"My God! He isn't going to stop," I screamed to nobody.

My world went into slow motion as I heard the grinding, crashing metal of the Ford tearing at the driver's door of my S-10, watching as the windshield ever so slowly crashed in on me. That would be the last I would remember until I awoke in the Med-Flight helicopter.

My youngest son would later relay most of the story to me, beginning with the fact that he had come upon the accident on his way home from work. A drunk driver traveling more than sixty-five miles per hour reported he had seen me coming but "thought he could beat me through the intersection." He didn't. The impact pushed my Chevy 107 feet up the highway, thirty-seven-and-a-half feet off the roadway, and flipped me around 180 degrees. A cap bolted on the bed of the truck had been "ripped" loose and thrown another fifty feet down the inter-section. As for me, the Jaws of Life were used to pry me from the mangled mess that used to be my pride and joy and I had gone into cardiac arrest twice at the scene.

My injuries were numerous with lacerations to my face and a severely broken hand—part of which later would be amputated due to the injury. I later was told that the medics commented on the fact they didn't know why I had on so many clothes but it was a good thing I did . . . the coveralls I mentioned earlier? They were too big for me; when I sat down, the collar came very high on my neck—the thickness of the collar, completely split in half, was credited with saving my life. It had prevented my jugular vein from being lacerated.

In the trauma area and later in my room, I kept asking for someone to please remove the cervical collar from my neck and clean the glass from under it; it was cutting my neck. The pain from the glass was so severe that I began to cry, but the attendants kept saying they couldn't remove it until test results were back; the pain was almost unbearable!

I had finally cried myself to sleep when, during the night, a nurse awakened me. Startled, I jumped. She placed her finger to her lips. *"Shh,"* she motioned and asked if my neck was still hurting. I shook my head "yes" and began to tear up again. She told me that, if I promised that I wouldn't move a muscle or say anything, she would remove the collar and clean the glass from my neck.

I whispered that I promised and she carefully and slowly began to remove the collar. When I started to say something, she said, *"Shh! You promised!"* She gently cleaned the glass from my wound, cleansed it with warm water, bandaged it, and replaced the collar.

"How is that, better?" she asked. I gave a slight nod and told her, "Much, much better." I thanked her and asked her name. "Kay," she responded as she smiled and turned to leave. Watching her go, I took note of her starched white uniform and white sweater. Her nursing shoes were spotless and not a wisp of her brown hair out of place under her starched white cap. She had worn a name tag but I had been unable to read it.

"Charlene, are you awake?" I asked the girl in the bed next to mine. Charlene had been a patient in the hospital for over three weeks due to complications from an earlier surgery and she knew every nurse on the floor. "Yeah," she replied.

"Who was that?" I asked. "She said her name is Kay but when does she work, what shift?"

"I've never seen her before!" Charlene answered. "But she sure was nice and so sweet and gentle!"

"Yeah," I said. "I hope she works in the morning."

Later that morning, another nurse and crew came in. "Excuse me! Could you please tell me what time and days Kay works?" I asked.

"Who?" she asked.

"Kay," I responded and went on to describe her in full detail.

"We have no 'Kay' here," she replied. Again, I described Kay and told her what had happened. "There is *NO KAY* here," she replied and whirled to go out the door.

They may not have had a Kay but I did. My own personal angel was sent to me from God to care for me and bring comfort when no other would.

The Rescue Angel

Randy DeMain

YEARS AGO I WAS IN SAIGON, VIETNAM, with a humanitarian aid group. We had been there about fourteen days, and I was ready to go home. On the way to the airport I had my airline ticket in my front shirt pocket. When I arrived, I got off the bus and entered the busy terminal to check in for my flight. People were everywhere. Somehow amid the crowds and all the bustling and jostling, I ended up inside the terminal with no ticket.

I checked and double-checked but nothing. No ticket.

I went into a mild panic; I was just so ready to be home. I went straight to the ticket counter and told the agent, "I've lost my ticket." I was sure he could look up my name on his computer and see that I did indeed have a ticket, and then print a duplicate for me to use to board the plane.

Unfortunately this was during the late 1990s when Vietnam was under a trade embargo and the airports there had little to no computer service. The airline agent had no ability to access my flight itinerary or ticket information.

He said, "I'm sorry, sir. I have no record of your flight or ticket. That will be two thousand five hundred dollars for your return flight home."

I was aghast. "You said two thousand five hundred dollars? Do you take credit cards?"

"No, sir. That's going to have to be cash."

Immediately I thought, *Okay, I'm stuck. I'm stuck in Vietnam.* I went over to the group of guys I was traveling with and told them, "We've got to do something. I'm stuck here. I've lost my ticket. I'm sure it was pilfered from my pocket on the way in."

So they all gathered around for a couple of minutes—a dozen guys huddled together. I prayed out loud, "Lord, I need my ticket home. Can You please tell me where to find it or restore this ticket?"

Then all the guys just dispersed and started looking around the airport for the ticket.

I turned around and had walked only about five steps when a man, a Vietnamese man, walked straight up to me and said, "Here's your ticket." I grabbed it and looked at it excitedly. And there, in fact, were my name and the day's date. They were my tickets! So I looked up to thank this gentleman, but he was not there. He was gone. Disappeared, literally.

Suddenly it dawned on me that this guy had been dressed in absolutely clean, perfectly pressed brown khaki shorts and a brown khaki shirt. He spoke to me in perfect English, with no Asian accent whatsoever. I knew he was indeed an angel and had brought me a new set of tickets, right there in the airport!

Angel in a White Suit
Shawn Bolz

WHEN I WAS SEVENTEEN YEARS OLD, I was babysitting two boys, Andrew and Jonathan, and I took them for a car ride. As I was starting to make a left turn, an old man who was driving too fast and wasn't paying attention hit our car.

Our car spun three times, and when it settled I heard a loud voice say, "Get the boys out of the car. You're okay." I looked next to me at Andrew, and he was okay, but the boy in the back, Jonathan, had been knocked unconscious. His seat belt was broken, and his head had gone through both the side window and the back window. He was knocked out and completely bloody.

Andrew, who was seven years old, was calling out, "Shawn! Shawn!" when I realized my legs were completely locked into where I was. Andrew continued, "Shawn, are we going to be okay?" and I said, "Yes, we are going to be okay, we are going to be okay"—even though at the time I had no reason to know that.

That's when a man dressed in a white suit walked up to the car. I have no idea where he could have come from because no one had stopped to help us at that point. Even the old man who hit us drove off. He came back later, but at that stage there was no one else around.

The man walked over to my broken window and said, "Get out of the car. Get Jonathan and Andrew out of the car. You are all going to be okay." I felt this inner strength come inside me, and I knew that what he was saying was true.

I said to him, "How do you know we are going to be okay though?"

He said, "Trust me. I'll go get help."

I turned and asked Andrew, "Can you get out of the car?' He was able to get out. Then I carried Jonathan, although I knew you are not supposed to move an injured person because they could have neck or back injuries. But I had a complete assurance that Jonathan was going to be okay.

I carried him out of the car and laid him on the grass. Not knowing what else to do, I called my parents, and then the paramedics arrived and drove us all in the ambulance to the hospital.

But here's the thing: by the time Jonathan got to the hospital, there were no cuts on his body. There was only one little cut on the back of his neck, but it could not have accounted for all the blood that was everywhere in the car and on his clothes.

These two little boys didn't believe in God at the time of the accident; in fact, they had no grid for whether God could heal or if angels were real. Yet Andrew asked me later, "Shawn, was that an angel that came up to our car?"

I didn't know Andrew had seen him—it happened so quickly.

I asked everybody who came to the scene, "Did you see this man? Did you see this man in a white suit?" But nobody saw him. He had told me he was going to a certain house to make a phone call, but the people at that house said they never saw him. Regardless, the paramedics got a call, and they came because of it.

And so not only was I not hurt, Andrew not hurt, and Jonathan not hurt, but I was also able to get out of the car—only by a miracle. We looked at the car later, and on my side and Jonathan's side the car was so crunched up that there was no way my legs could have been pulled out. And if Jonathan had really gone through the two windows that way, then there is no way I should have been able to remove him and for him to still have been okay.

I believe we were saved by an angel—an angel in a white suit.

Do Angels Wear Sweatshirts?

Janice Asien LaRosa

WHEN THE DOCTOR'S OFFICE at my annual heart checkup asked what phone number they could reach me at the next day, I gave them my mother's number because daughters, Sarah, eight, and Joy, four, and I would probably be over at Mom's, like we were most days.

Fourteen years ago, I had open-heart surgery, when I was a young, twenty-two-year-old newlywed. Since that time, I had never really felt the improvement my heart surgeon had expected me to feel. I shrugged off the always-tired feeling I had, chalking it up to the fact that I was a busy mom of two young children. All the moms I knew shared how tired they felt all the time. So I wasn't worried while I awaited the results from routine heart tests.

I'd told my husband, Bob, to join us at my mom's for dinner after he got home from work.

Just as he was walking in the front door, the phone rang.

"I'm sorry, Janice," I recognized the voice as my doctor, "I'm uncomfortable with what I see on your tests. I think the large hole in your heart has opened, or maybe was never fully closed with your first surgery. Regardless, we're looking at another open-heart surgery."

After hanging up the phone, I sat stunned on the couch. It was one thing being a newlywed and fearing I would make my new husband of one month and one day a widower; it was a whole other thing now: I was petrified at the thought of possibly dying and leaving my two little girls without a mom!

"What's wrong?" Bob asked.

My mom walked over to the couch wiping her hands on a dishtowel. "Janice, honey, please? What did they say?"

"How can this be happening again? They think the hole in my heart is open again!" I sobbed to Bob. "I've never felt like this, but I feel like just running away!"

"Let's do it! Let's go, just for tonight, let's take the kids, you come too," he said, turning to my mom and taking my hand.

"We can't do that, can we?" I asked.

"Why not? Nothing will be any different in just one day! Let's take the girls away and all have a night of fun and for just a few hours pretend we never heard this news today. Tomorrow we'll come home and face what we have to but not tonight, come on!" Bob said.

"This is crazy . . . but let's go!" I said, jumping up from the couch.

We threw a few things in a small suitcase and drove about thirty minutes away to a pretty hotel and checked in. But in the middle of the night, while everyone lay sleeping, I lay staring up at the dark ceiling, unable to sleep. It was as if a thick cloak gripped me and all I kept picturing was my two precious girls, navigating life without a mother's love and guidance.

I reached my hand over the side of the bed and quietly slid the nightstand drawer open, feeling around for the Bible. I tiptoed to the bathroom, turned on the light, and closed it so just a slit of light came through the door. I opened the Bible, reading the first verse I saw, lit with a ray of light: Revelation 5:5, "The Lion of the tribe of Judah . . . has triumphed."

I gasped, because since I was around ten, and first saw *Born Free*, I absolutely fell in love with lions, but not until that moment had I ever once thought of Jesus as a lion!

I decided there and then that no matter what I felt or faced from that moment forward I was going to hold on to that verse. I found and bought a poster with a majestic lion on it with that verse, and I taped it on to my bedroom door. During the day, I painted on a brave face for my family, but at night, fear seemed to engulf me. Each time I was afraid, I'd stand in front of the poster and draw on the comfort and peace I desperately needed.

My heart surgeon told my husband and me that going into a chest for the second time because of scarring and adhesions having formed from the first surgery would mean much heavier bleeding during surgery so they would use fresh platelets to help control and lessen the bleeding.

"Can I donate platelets to my wife?" Bob asked.

"Sure, that would be great," the surgeon said. "We'll harvest those from you the morning before the surgery."

The morning came for me to be admitted to the hospital; my surgery was scheduled for the next day. I took the poster off my bedroom closet and rolled it up. "This can hang on the wall in my room next to the pictures of the girls," I said to Bob.

We drove Sarah and Joy to my mom's house with their suitcases. We all were so used to being with each other, I knew Sarah and Joy would be very comfortable at their gramma's.

"Mommy and Daddy love you both so much. Have a fun day with Gramma," I said, walking quickly to the door so they wouldn't see my tears.

The part of the hospital where Bob donated platelets was in a building across the street from the main hospital. It took a few hours; I watched as a tube of blood came out of Bob's arm and went into a machine behind him, spinning the red blood and what looked like liquid gold, filling a container. The blood went through another tube, and into his other arm.

Afterward, as we crossed the street and headed back to the main hospital, the sidewalks were filled with people. My eyes fixed on one woman coming directly toward me. I read the rather large words on the front of her white sweatshirt as she got closer: *The lion of the tribe of Judah has triumphed.* I stopped and spun around.

"Bob, did you see that?" I asked, stunned. "That woman, her sweatshirt said my Scripture!"

"Wow, that's cool!" Bob said.

"Cool, yes, but way more than that, it's God showing me, telling me, He is with me!" I said, not moving, still staring in the direction she walked.

"Come on, we've got to get to Admitting," he said, gently tugging at my arm.

I continued to talk about the woman in the sweatshirt. After a while Bob just smiled politely at my constant repeating of what it meant to me.

"Of all the Scriptures, of all the days to see that . . . ," I continued as the doors opened to our floor on the heart unit. We stepped forward to leave the elevator and I noticed the color leave Bob's face. I looked to see what had caught his attention and there standing right in front of us with other people waiting to get on the elevator was the same woman.

As everyone pushed forward to get on the elevator, I said, "I'll be right back, I've got to tell her," I said, looking at Bob.

"Go . . . ," he said, his hand waving me forward, dropping down hard onto a bench against the wall still with a shocked look on his face.

I reached my hand through the crowd to touch her shoulder. "Excuse me . . . ," I said, trying to stop her, but as my hand moved down to touch her shoulder, she wasn't there. My eyes darted back and forth and I pulled my arm back as the elevator doors closed.

"What . . . ?" I looked around. The hall was empty, except for Bob and me. He patted the bench seat and slid over. I sat down next to him. We both said nothing. He raised his eyebrows, shaking his head back and forth. "Okay then . . . okay," he said, taking my hand and drawing in a deep breath. "Ready?"

"I'm ready now," I said as both of us stood and walked to my room.

Postscript: The large hole in Janice's heart was successfully closed.

The Travel Agent Angel

Doug Addison

ABOUT TEN YEARS AGO, I went with a group of people to Seoul, South Korea, to study the effects of church growth and church prayer. Some of the largest churches in the world were in South Korea then. There were about twenty of us in this group.

We didn't go as a tour group or as an official group of any kind. We went over on our own. So when we arrived in Seoul, there wasn't anyone to pick us up or organize anything for us. We just flew in, and there we were.

Well, pretty quickly there was a lot of confusion. Twenty of us from the San Francisco Bay area all arrived to find ourselves totally lost. There we were, with all our luggage, overwhelmed. Frankly, most of us were almost in tears. We didn't know where to go or how to get there.

Fortunately, a Korean travel agent named Sue, who spoke perfect English, summoned us. She came over and started waving for all of us to get on the bus that was waiting for us. It was air-conditioned, and she brought each of us water, which was great because we all were parched. She rode with us as far as the bus could go, then she told us the bus wouldn't be going farther because the local streets were too narrow.

So she got us all off the bus, got all of our luggage, and hailed five or six taxis for us. She handed each of us notes written in Korean for the cab drivers so they would know where to take us. And off we went.

The next day we told the people we were staying with, "Hey, thanks. That was cool to send the travel agent and the bus for us." But no one had done that. No one had organized anything for us.

A few days later we all were back in the middle of Seoul, a city of more than nine million people at that time, and we were completely lost again. Some people in our group had gotten separated from us, and we didn't know where to go or what we were doing. Our travel agent, Sue, was there again to get us back together and help us.

On the last day we were visiting a folk center way outside of town. The pastor who was with us was a diabetic. He had gotten separated from the group and became very sick. He actually started going into diabetic shock and losing his sight. But he started to come out of the shock and come to, and when he did, he looked up and Sue was suddenly there. She told him, "Your group is over there. They are over there." Then she kind of pushed him over toward us, and we found him and were able to help him. Sue, however, just went away.

Everyone in that group is convinced to this day that Sue was an angel, cloaked in clothing as a person. She was there to save our lives.

Messenger at Sunset

Marci Alborghetti

FOUR MONTHS AFTER MY SECOND MELANOMA was removed, I headed to Key West for the winter. I felt that God had blessed me: the type of cancer I had could be excised, and although I would require monitoring for the rest of my life, I was considered cured. (*Thank You, God!*)

I'd spent a week in Key West earlier, falling in love with the light, color, and buzz on the island. So when the doctor reluctantly okayed the trip, I decided that God had cleared my flight plan.

And it was, literally, a flight plan. I was fleeing issues of mortality, cancer, and my suddenly different future. I couldn't bear another cold, bleak Connecticut winter, just me and my mordant fears fighting it out in my apartment that over-looked a hospital.

I was determined to go. I would stick with my precancer plan of returning to Key West for the winter, *no matter what!* My diagnosis, and subsequent consul-tations with doctors who all agreed that I would likely spend the rest of my life fighting this illness, had tipped my world, and I wasn't sure how to set it right again. I was desperate to make just one thing go the way I'd planned it.

From the beginning, all of my careful plans were like so many pick-up-sticks tossed into the air to land anywhere but where I'd planned. My plane had to make an unscheduled stop, and I was exhausted by the time I got to the room and bath I'd rented sight unseen from a very nice-sounding lady. The flamingo-pink taxi left me in front of a house that resembled something out of a gothic nightmare. Dark and looming, the ancient structure was covered with vines and vegetation. A filthy, mold-filled pool in the back (the pool I'd been told about and had imagined myself lounging around daily under a sunshade) looked like it hadn't been cleaned in decades. My "room and bath" was a space separated from the rest of the house with a sliding wall so flimsy you could hear a mosquito sneeze on the other side.

For the first time, I let myself believe I'd made a terrible mistake. For the first time since my diagnosis, I started to realize that maybe I wasn't in charge.

The next day I searched for another rental. My expectations, and my courage, waned with each passing hour. By the time the last place I'd circled in the newspaper came up, my whole world was caving in on me. Whatever plans I'd had for this trip, or my life for that matter, were no longer real even to me.

The last place was perfect: a lovely little cottage behind a pretty gate two streets down from the main drag, Duval Street, yet quiet and shaded. When the landlord and his wife told me they wanted a yearlong renter, I sat on their front steps and cried. The whole garbled story came pouring out, and in ten minutes, they'd offered me a four-month rental and were helping me move in.

As hard as it is to create a "routine" in Key West, old habits die even harder, and soon I was on a regular schedule. Rise, pray, walk, write, sunset. Sunset, as anyone who's been to Key West knows, is an Occasion. People travel from all over the world to experience this carnival of color, music, art, and entertainment that sets up each evening with street performers of every kind. A perfect winter evening can draw thousands of tourists and snow-birds like me off beaches and porches to witness the controlled chaos. It's even rowdier during spring break when college students show up to give cash to the hotels and bars and *agita* to the residents, most of whom never go near Duval Street in March.

Nor was I a fan of the spring-breakers. Many were loud, messy, drunk, and generally obnoxious. But I wasn't about to let a bunch of wild children interrupt my routine. So on a Wednesday in March, I dutifully trudged to the sunset, grimly determined to take my usual perch on a large, stone planter from which I could watch the sun go down. I would enjoy myself at any cost.

I grew more upset as I walked. The streets teemed with kids enjoying themselves. I saw their perfect, beautiful, unscarred bodies, and the joy they took in themselves. The doctors had told me that—at best—I'd be having biopsies for the rest of my life. I mentally compared my solitary, compartmentalized life, complete with a body that would come to look like a tic-tac-toe board, to the time of their lives these kids were having. And I lost.

Then I saw some kid sitting on my stone planter.

That was it. The tears started, and I almost turned and went back to my dim, quiet cottage. But something about him caught my attention. He looked different for one thing, not like most of the half-clad kids running around. Indeed, for an 80-degree evening, he was remarkably overdressed. I looked more closely.

Despite the heat, he wore cargo pants, an untucked, white oxford shirt, and immaculately clean work boots. But it was his hat that made me smile: one of those old-fashioned, heavy canvas, olive-colored hats . . . with ear flaps. He wasn't sweating at all; in fact, he exuded an oasis of calm that drew me in and, somehow, included me. He sat cross-legged, self-contained, serenely observing everything around us. When he saw me, he wordlessly reached down a hand to hoist me up beside him.

After a surprisingly comfortable silence, I asked him what school he attended, and he answered in a soft Southern drawl. He was studying environmental science and was quite focused on what was becoming an exceptionally beautiful sunset.

He began to cheerfully explain all the flaws that would make this sunset so extraordinary. There were atmospheric factors marring the sky's clarity, thus, the prospective sunset would offer intensely vibrant colors.

Just before the sun touched the horizon, he grabbed my hand. Startled, I looked at him. His green eyes were brimming. "I can't bear to watch," he said softly. "It's just too beautiful." He leaped dramatically off the planter and gave me one last look before vanishing into the crowd. "Isn't it?" he asked.

I turned back to the horizon and watched as the dipping sun projected every color of the rainbow, and then some, even after it had disappeared. I sat there long after others had returned to the Duval Street bars and restaurants. As I watched the spring-breakers, they didn't seem like the same spoiled brats who had irritated me all week. One girl looked sad and uncertain, straggling behind a larger group. A tall, thin boy was helping a drunken friend maneuver through the crowd. A young couple holding hands lingered almost as long as I, watching the sky shade from magenta to indigo to darkness.

My fingers grazed the scar on my leg from my last surgery. The indentation was still there, and if it hadn't been dark, I knew I would see the caterpillar-like line. Flawed. Just like the sky that had produced this magnificent sunset.

I searched for the green-eyed boy during sunsets long after spring break ended. Of course I never found him; he'd done what he'd been sent to do in our short time together. In the nearly twenty years since, life has confirmed the gift he gave me that night, the truth that I started understanding the moment he disappeared: despite its many flaws and plans gone awry, my life has enormous beauty and an order I can't even begin to comprehend. I'm not meant to.

Reason's last step is the recognition that there are

an infinite number of things which are beyond it.

—Blaise Pascal

CHAPTER 5

Heard in Our Hearts

And having been warned in a dream not to go back to Herod,

they returned to their country by another route.

When they had gone, an angel of the Lord appeared to Joseph in

a dream. "Get up," he said, "take the child and his mother and

escape to Egypt. Stay there until I tell you, for Herod is going

to search for the child to kill him."

—MATTHEW 2:12–13 (NIV)

The Angels of Hemby Hospital
Natalie Hullander

AFTER MY THREE-YEAR-OLD SON, ZAC, was diagnosed with leukemia, I had questions for the doctors—and for God. *Will You keep Zac safe? Will he be okay?*

Zac checked into Hemby Children's Hospital in Charlotte, North Carolina. One night he had a seizure. All my fears came to the surface.

When I finally fell asleep in the hospital room, I dreamed there were many children surrounding me. One little boy had chicken pox. Some kids were giggling. "Do you have any candy?" one little girl asked. The children told me they had died in this hospital, but they all seemed happy and pain free as they played peacefully together.

I woke with a start, but soon felt calm. Those children wanted me to know that whether Zac stayed here with our family or went to join another one in heaven, he'd be okay.

The next morning I called my sister. "You saw the angels of Hemby Hospital," she said. "There are stories in the news about them." Many people had seen angels at this hospital. Mine appeared as children.

It took three years, but Zac made it through his leukemia battle. And I've no doubt there were angels by his side—and mine—all the time.

River Angel

William Thatcher

SINCE SUNUP I'D BEEN OUT on the Missouri River, riding around in my fourteen-foot metal boat. The river was running high and fast, swollen from heavy fall rains. Lots of debris floated past, mainly branches from the willow trees that grew along the shore. Every once in a while an entangled mess would come my way, and I'd have to maneuver around it. But I was used to the outdoors, and to adventure—small boats, single-engine planes, hiking in nature. I liked excitement, and I liked that God always made sure I came home safe. This evening I would thank Him properly over a fresh duck dinner with my wife.

As I motored along, the sun was high in a bright blue sky. A raccoon at the water's edge took a little dip. A doe slipped quickly, silently through the trees. Nature was abundantly on display, but I had not come across one other boat the whole day.

"Bill!" The call startled me. Who had snuck up on my boat like that?

I turned around and looked in every direction. Hunters don't play games. There was no one out here on the river. No one but me. Just as I'd suspected. But still, I could have sworn I heard my name, clear as day.

"Bill!"

This time the call came with more urgency. It was a warning call. Unmistakably.

I jerked around to look over my shoulder. *Whoa!* An enormous log barreled straight toward me. I turned the motor and swerved my little boat out of its path. Seconds later it passed by me. The log must have been twenty feet long and three feet wide. Probably washed away from one of the dams upriver. About one hundred yards downstream was an empty steel barge moored along the shore. The log hit the steel barge so hard and fast that the barge was launched up into the air before finally falling back into the water. *That could have been me!*

I could barely catch my breath. My hands were shaking so hard I couldn't hold on to the motor. If I hadn't moved out of that log's path, I knew I'd be dead.

That night when I got home from my latest adventure, I had more than our dinner to thank the Lord for. "I heard an angel out on the river today," I told my wife. "An angel called my name—and saved my life."

In My Mind's Eye

Karen Lorimer

HEAVY FOG SHROUDED THE MOUNTAINTOP. I stood there, my feet just inches from the edge, peering down below. The forest was barely visible through the mist, the treetops swayed with the howling wind.

Suddenly, someone came from behind and covered my eyes.

Terrified, I froze. "Please, let me see!" I begged.

"It's okay, my child," a woman whispered. "Be calm and you will see what is before you." Her voice was soft. Melodic. *Otherworldly.* It instantly calmed me. I couldn't see her, yet somehow, almost involuntarily, I trusted her.

I took a deep breath, then another. Ever so slowly, my muscles relaxed. Then the woman gently pulled her hands away from my eyes. It was like I had supernatural vision. Everything was beautiful! The fog had disappeared. The sky was now a vivid sapphire. Golden rays washed over the forest. I turned around . . . and that's when I saw her wings.

She was an angel. Statuesque and beautiful, with long, flowing wheat-colored hair. I'd never felt so safe, so protected.

I woke with a jolt. *What a dream!* I thought. I'd always had a big faith but what was *that* all about?

Puzzled, I got ready for work. Lately I'd been putting in extra hours at a ceramics factory to save for my upcoming wedding. I called my fiancé, Jeffrey, before I left and told him about the dream. "What do you think it means?"

"Maybe God just wants to remind you that He and His angels are always with you," Jeffrey said.

That sounded good to me. By the time I got to work, I'd pushed the dream out of my mind. We had a busy day ahead making molds. Carefully, I lined up the levers on my machine—if they weren't even, the boiling ceramic liquid would overflow. I crouched down and got eye-level to make sure the levers were perfectly aligned. I pressed start.

Bam! The scorching liquid exploded, shooting straight into my eyes. "Help!" I screamed. "It burns!"

My boss rushed me to the hospital. With every passing second, the ceramic cooled, sealing my eyes shut. In the ER I shook uncontrollably from the shock. "Please don't let me go blind!" I begged the doctor. I thought of my wedding . . . my life . . .

The doctor ordered me a sedative. "I know it's hard," he said, "but just try to stay calm."

Calm. All at once I remembered those words: "Be calm and you will see what is before you." The angel's heavenly voice echoed in my mind. And as if I were standing back on that mountain, my entire body relaxed into the dreamscape. I felt safe, totally protected. I turned down the sedative.

Little by little, the doctor removed the ceramic, revealing slivers of sight. Soon I could see completely.

"There seems to be no permanent damage," the doctor said. "You've got great luck." But two months later, as I walked down the aisle toward Jeffrey on our wedding day, I knew it was much more than that.

Nothing to Fear

Lois Halley

BEDTIME WAS MISERABLE FOR ME when I was seven. The attic door just outside my bedroom had an unfriendly habit of creaking open by itself in the night, and I was sure that it was because of some bone-chilling monster on its way out to get me.

"It's an old house, Lois," my mother explained as she tucked me in one night. "The hinges on that door are all rusted, and you know how drafty it can get." But her soothing words were no match for my wild imagination.

"Can you read to me to help me go to sleep?" I asked. Mom sat by my bedside and read me a story, and another, and another, until I finally dozed off, my stuffed tiger, Mumsy, clutched securely to my chest.

During the day, the attic was anything but frightening. The very next afternoon my friends and I ran up and down its steps for fun. First they were a mountain to climb. Then a ship's mast. Then a magnificent castle staircase. "See, Mumsy," I said, climbing over boxes and furniture we'd stored. "There's nothing scary here."

But when night fell, everything changed. The attic's rough wooden floors and unfinished walls were dimly lit by bare bulbs that made everything look haunted. Those piles of storage boxes and old furniture took on more sinister shapes. What could be lurking in the shadows of the crawl space? I was terrified I was going to find out.

"You played up there all day—you know that there's nothing to worry about," Mom reassured me that night, kissing me on the forehead. "You have Mumsy here to keep an eye on things, don't you?"

"I guess so," I said. Mom was right. Mumsy was a fierce tiger, after all, proud and unafraid. I hugged him and closed my eyes. Mom left me to my bedtime prayers and dreams.

This night, I found myself dreaming of a beautiful woman standing by my bedroom door. She was draped in blue-and-white silk that flowed to the floor in ethereal pleats. It was still night and my room was pitch-black, but I could see her clearly. She illuminated everything around her. Smiling, she offered me her hand. I climbed out of bed and took it, my other hand keeping a tight grasp on Mumsy.

Together, the three of us went up the attic stairs. The woman guided me to every corner of the attic. She even showed me the crawl space. Her glowing presence banished the shadows. She never spoke, but I understood that she was showing me there was nothing to fear. With that angel by my side, the attic looked just like it did during the day—a place where I could feel safe to imagine and play.

My mother woke me up the next morning. "Where did Mumsy get to?" she asked. I searched under the covers, under my pillow, under my bed. My tiger was nowhere to be found. Remembering my dream, I hopped out of bed and raced up the attic stairs. There, waiting for me on the top step, was Mumsy!

Eventually I got old enough to sleep without a tiger guard. And today I have an attic filled with my own boxes and old furniture. But I still say my bedtime prayers and rely on angels to shine light on my fears.

May Wind

Florence B. Smith

WHEN HE WAS SIX, David was put in a full leg cast, the result of an operation we hoped would enable him to walk normally. Struck with spinal meningitis when he was three months old, he had been left completely deaf and severely retarded. Doctors were blunt with his father and me about the outlook for David: "He won't be capable of grasping abstract concepts, and his attention span will never exceed about two minutes."

None of that affected David's charm though. Nor his ability to communicate with us. He learned to use signs and gestures; David's grunts and sounds became our language.

One night, because of the uncomfortable cast, David was cross and restless. His legs itched. I tried lullabies and stories, but my usual sleepy-time tricks weren't working. David couldn't seem to settle down. It was an exceptionally calm May night, so I opened windows throughout the house. *Maybe the fresh air will soothe him.*

Finally, struggling with his cast, I carried David to my room. "You're getting too big," I groaned teasingly. He giggled when I dropped him on the bed. "Now you close those eyes." I gently patted his side.

David squeezed his eyes shut, then popped them open again, wanting to play. Something caught his attention, and he pointed to a picture on the wall, near my chest of drawers. "Who?" he signed.

"That's Jesus," I replied.

"Where he live?"

I was surprised by his question. He'd never been curious about Jesus before, and I had little hope that he would ever grasp the concept of God.

"Where Jesus live?" David repeated. I pointed up to heaven.

David looked at the ceiling and back at me, puzzled. *He's really trying to understand.* I raised the window blind and pointed at the ink-blue sky. Lifting himself on one skinny elbow, David craned his neck from the bed to look out. Something told me to go on with my lesson.

"Jesus lives up there," I said. "In heaven with the angels." David watched me intently, then his eyes searched the night sky. I breathed in the sweet, calm air. "Someday you will go to heaven," I continued. "Jesus will have the angels fix your body. You will walk as well as Mother, your ears won't be broken, and you will be able to talk perfectly."

"Why I not see Jesus?"

My heart skipped a beat. How to answer my child?

At that instant, out of the still night came a powerful blast of wind. The windowpanes shook and rattled. I screamed and David nearly jumped off the bed. The blind flapped against the window frame; the curtains billowed. I clasped my arms around David and turned my face away. *Blam!* The bedroom door slammed shut. Then, as quick as the wind had stirred up, it stopped. We sat in the still silence. All was peaceful again.

David wiggled out of my grip to look at me, his blue eyes wide. A broad smile swept across his face, and he lifted his arms and flapped them as if he were flying. "Jesus," he signed, pointing upward and laughing, bouncing on the bed. He wanted me to pack his suitcase so he could fly to heaven right then!

As best I could, I explained that Jesus would come for him when Jesus was ready, not when David wanted to go. David turned serious. He gazed out into the quiet night and blew a kiss toward heaven.

"Who is the kiss for?" I asked.

David pretended his arms were wings and flapped them. Then he lay down and fell fast asleep, peaceful as a baby.

As the years have passed, David, though still handicapped, has exceeded everyone's expectations. He mows the lawn and helps his father do handiwork around the house. My husband says David knows the precise tool to hand him even before it is requested. David also has a fascination with outboard motors, and understands the intricate details of dozens of different models. He has taught himself to type, and keeps up a correspondence with some of the outboard-motor manufacturers. He also loves to wash dishes (he volunteers at the American Legion food kitchen one night a week), and he brings me coffee in bed every morning without fail.

When a gust blows, David searches the sky curiously. He repeats the story of his "wind angel" and reminds me that someday Jesus is going to come for him and fix his body. "And I will be able to talk in heaven," he signs. I know the story he will tell. The story of the night God allowed something to capture his attention and never let go.

Two Minutes to Live

Dennis T. Jodouin

I USED TO THINK I was lucky. As a lieutenant in the Toledo, Ohio, fire depart-ment I've had water-laden ceilings fall on my head, I've been blown down by explosions, I've fallen through floors eaten by fire. But after December 5, I've had to question how much was really luck. Maybe my mother was right when she told us children that each of us had his own guardian angel.

At Engine House No. 19 on that particular December morning, we checked our equipment as usual, paying special attention to our face masks. Smoke is the firefighter's principal enemy, and we always make sure every valve is working, every air tank full. Then, at 10:43 AM, the alarm sounded. As our pumper raced to the call at Chestnut and Noble, I wondered if everyone had got out safely. If they had, our job was to try to save the building.

Our truck approached the corner. Other pumpers were laying in hoses from a hydrant, their crews stretching the lines to the front and rear of the frame duplex. Just as we pulled up, a violent back draft explosion blew out the building's store-front window. Glass flew onto the crumbling concrete stoop. Black, rolling smoke vented from the hole. I ordered my crew to mask up.

We were beginning to pull the hose off the pumper when the chief ran over to me. "Get upstairs quick, Lieutenant!" he said. "Use the back way. There's been screaming reported coming from up there."

Now it was a different ball game: We were no longer just fighting a fire; we were looking for a person trapped inside. I looked around at our new man, Bill.

"Let's go," I said. On the way, because he was a rookie, I briefed him. We'd climb the outside stairs, gain entrance to the second floor, and feel our way through the smoke in the upstairs apartment, looking for a survivor. "Remember your training now," I said, little thinking that within moments I'd forget my own seventeen years of experience.

We raced up the outside stairs to the landing, paused, slipped on the face-pieces of our masks, and turned on the valves. There was a hiss as compressed air flowed from the tank on my back through the tube into my mask. We'd have about twenty minutes before the air gave out.

"Okay, stay close to me," I said to Bill, my voice sounding muffled as it came through the mask's speaking diaphragm. We headed inside.

The first room we came to was filled with black, black smoke. I switched on my hand light. It didn't begin to penetrate the darkness. Following procedure, I started moving to my right, feeling my way around the wall. A stove, a refrigerator, and then an empty space. A doorway!

"Wait," I said, talking into the smoke. I could hardly see Bill. We stopped and listened, but the only sound was the muffled noise of firefighters from the street below.

Our proper procedure was clear. Crouching into a semicrawl, we went through the doorway into the room off the kitchen, keeping contact with the wall on our right. I kept locating the wall with my foot, then I stretched into the middle of the room feeling for a human form. I touched pieces of furniture: a sofa, a chair, a cabinet. Then, on the floor, a heap of clothes. Was that a body? No, just clothes.

A bright blur ahead. A window. With the butt of my hand light I burst the glass; a surge of black smoke rushed past me into the open. I kept on. *Wheeze. Wheeze.* I could hear Bill behind me, drawing air into his mask.

Perspiration was running in a steady stream down my face and neck, stinging my eyes. The intense heat on my neck was a constant reminder that the fire was getting closer, racing up inside the walls. I skirted a bookcase, came to a corner, turned left, following the wall. Inch by inch I groped in the darkness, searching for what, I didn't know. Except for our own wheezing breath, I hadn't heard a sound in the apartment since we began the search. Now little orange fragments started falling from the ceiling. Bad news. The fire was so hot it had ignited the plaster. Bits and pieces of it were floating down from the ceiling like deadly fireflies. I touched the wall again. Even through my gloves it was hot. We had to hurry!

Suddenly I wasn't getting enough air. I inhaled more deeply. My tank couldn't be empty—we hadn't been in the building ten minutes. The warning bell in my equipment hadn't rung. I remembered procedure, reached for the emergency bypass valve, and cranked it two turns. Nothing.

"Bill," I yelled into the blackness, "I've got trouble with my air." I tried to keep my muffled voice calm, but I heard a trace of panic in it. Without air, I had one, at the most two minutes to live.

And then I made my first mistake. I did something totally against procedure; I ignored the first rule of safety for the firefighter: Use the buddy system. In an emergency, you can share your partner's supply of air until you are out of danger. But instead I ordered the rookie fireman away. "Go back the way we came and get me another tank," I shouted. "I'll meet you at the landing."

Bill had scarcely left when I began to choke. Now panic took an iron hold and I made my second mistake. My only thought was to get air. The quickest way was to go straight to the door without circling the wall as I should have done. I stood up and ran.

I bumped into a table. A sofa. Another table. I ran forward, hit a chair, turned back, grasped my valve, and turned it again. Nothing. My lungs burned. I sucked harder but there was just no air. Where was that door? Words came from training: "Don't forget," the drill instructors had preached, "you always have air trapped inside your clothing."

Gasping, I fell to the floor, disconnected my inhalation tube from the oxygen tank, and stuck it inside my coat. Praying. A few more moments of life. Let there be air inside my fire coat!

I sucked hard. A precious bit of air came through! The smoke tasted hot, acrid, but the air was still breathable. I had bought another minute. I forced myself back up on to my hands and knees and started crawling through the obstacle course, under a table, over a stuffed chair. There was no way out now and I knew it. I started crying. With the same strange logic I had used in sending Bill away, I blamed God for my mistakes. Over and over the thought repeated itself, irrationally, insistently: *Dear God, why are You doing this to me? You know I'm getting married soon. I have so much to live for!*

Then I heard the voice, a whisper: *"Look up! Look up!"*

I barely moved my head, turning to the right. The voice came again, more insistently, *"Not to your right, look to your left!"*

The voice came more clearly now, as if through a megaphone in my ear, pressuring me as I felt my reactions slowing down. *"To your left. Look up to your left! Don't you see it?"*

Yes, I saw it! Through the blackness I barely made out a small fuzzy zone of light.

In slow motion I got up and started toward it, stumbling, falling. The light became a faint outline, then a distinct form. It was a window. The same window I had burst earlier.

I ripped off my mask and forced my body halfway through the frame into the fresh air outside. Again and again I drew clean air into my lungs, relishing the sounds of men below.

Then Bill was at my side. He helped me down the stairs to the street, where I learned that the trouble with my equipment was a faulty valve. The cry from inside the building had been a cat, which had not escaped. But not one person's life was lost—including my own!

When my mother used to tell me about my guardian angel, she had good scriptural backing. Jesus says about children, "I tell you that their angels in heaven always see the face of my Father in heaven" (Matthew 18:10, NIV).

Does a child's angel stay with him always, constantly regarding the face of the Father . . . even when, as an adult, he may forget to look up to God?

Today that is a question I no longer ask. I am satisfied it was my own angel who whispered to me, *"Look up!"*

Reason to Go On
Mark Smith

I DIDN'T TAKE VERY GOOD CARE of myself after my wife died. I slept erratically, ate junk food, cut myself off from friends. One night I flopped into bed, not even bothering to unmake it. I couldn't believe she was gone after battling a host of medical problems. It should have been me. I stared at the ceiling and thought back to my past—the dark years of my addiction, and the girl who changed everything.

I was at my lowest point yet, sitting on the hardwood floor of my one-room apartment in the roughest part of town. I'd spent the past four years deep into drugs and alcohol. Burned every bridge, lost faith in God, and stolen from my mother. I thought about getting clean sometimes, but I always went right back to using.

What was the point of anything? I looked around. The sink overflowed with dishes. I couldn't remember the last time I'd taken out the trash. I felt stuck in a cage of my own making, like I was too far gone, beyond help.

I put my head in my hands and sat there, my heart pounding in my ears. As I raised my head I had the overwhelming sense that I wasn't alone. Light danced before my eyes. I turned—a girl was sitting right beside me. *Karen?* I rubbed my eyes in disbelief. She was my best friend in high school. We'd lost touch years ago but I could see her clearly—her big smile, those green eyes. *You're just seeing things,* I told myself. *Going through withdrawal.* Then she faded away.

I glanced at the phone. I still had Karen's number somewhere. What if I called her? What did I have to lose?

"Hi," I said, fumbling with the cord. "Is this Karen?" I thought she might hang up when she recognized my voice. I couldn't blame her.

"Yes," she said. She paused. "Mark, is that you?"

"It's me." I waited for the click.

"Hey there, stranger. Good to hear your voice again."

She didn't hang up. In fact, she seemed happy to talk to me. I opened up. Told her about my struggles getting sober. My falling-out with my mom. She listened, made me laugh even. It felt like old times.

Karen and I used to see a lot of each other. Her best friend was dating my best friend, and somehow we'd just clicked from the beginning. I wondered why I hadn't kept up with her, but that was only one mistake I'd made among many. I told Karen I was done making mistakes.

"I believe you," she said.

If Karen could believe me, maybe I could believe in myself too. Right there on the phone I resolved to stay clean. From then on, anytime I felt that self-destructive itch, I called Karen. Whenever I hesitated about the daunting tasks ahead—reaching out to my mom, finding a job—Karen reassured me. "Faith helps," she said one day. "When is the last time you spoke to God?"

Karen was right. It had been too long. I started praying again and got the courage to call my mom. She was willing to give me a second chance! I moved home and invited Karen over to have dinner with us.

"They're looking for warehouse help where I work," Karen said. I'd done that kind of work before. The next day, I took the bus to the industrial supply house and filled out an application. Karen winked from the receptionist's desk. A week later, I had a job.

I'd forgotten how much I loved working. Even better, Karen and I carpooled. She did the driving, I paid for the gas.

We started to have lunch together, then dinners out. After a short time "officially dating," we married. We had eighteen years together as husband and wife. Happy years I might never have lived to see if not for Karen. I still couldn't believe God had put such an angel in my life. Why had He taken her away?

I lay uncomfortably on top of the bed and played back the memory reel like some movie gone wrong. Karen's stroke, her downward spiral. After she passed away, I'd tried holding things together, but it was no use. How could I go on without her encouragement? I hadn't felt so hopeless since those dark days of my addiction, when Karen came back into my life. I dozed fitfully, dreaming of Karen.

The next morning I woke up with a terrible knot in my stomach. I rolled to my side and winced in pain. White light danced before my eyes, and I had a vaguely familiar feeling. *This has happened before,* I thought. *I didn't dream it then, and I'm not dreaming it now.* I wasn't alone.

In the light, Karen's face appeared crystal clear, just like the last time. But she wasn't smiling. Her green eyes brimmed over with tears.

"Why are you crying?"

"You're not well," she said. "Get to the hospital."

The knot in my stomach tightened. Something wasn't right. I did as Karen said and dragged myself out of bed. I could hardly breathe by the time I walked into the ER. "I think I'm having a heart attack," I said.

One look at me told the staff I was in trouble. I had surgery the next day—a quintuple heart bypass. It was that serious. But I survived. Again. Thanks to two perfectly timed visions that could only have come from heaven above. Visions of my angel, Karen, who wants the best for me on earth. Now I live every day to my fullest potential, here and now, nourishing body and soul till the day we will be reunited.

The Nutmeg Angel
Delores E. Topliff

SOMETIMES GOD KEEPS US FROM HARM even before we know we need protection. When my sons were five and seven, I was a single mom working hard to support my family. I cherished every moment we could be together and made sure nothing took away family time on weekends—except church. Weekends were our times to putter around the garden, make good smells come from the oven, and do all the projects that make a house a home. I carefully managed all other errands, including grocery shopping, on Monday through Friday, on the way to or from work or after picking the kids up from school and daycare each day. Nothing interfered with weekends.

Except one Saturday I felt the strongest urge to bake a custard pudding. I was suddenly totally starving for it. I could see and smell the fragrant nutmeg sprinkled on top, almost taste its perfect eggnog flavor and smooth-textured goodness. I told my boys and they clamored with excitement as they went outside to play. But I soon found my pantry had run out of nutmeg. There wasn't a single grain of it in the house.

What's custard without nutmeg? I guess it could be done, but the results would be disappointing in my books. The urging came stronger than ever. I had to bake that custard, today. The nudge was strong enough to break my forever pattern. We would go to the store right now, on a Saturday.

I called in the boys from the front yard where seven-year-old Andrew was teaching five-year-old Aaron to wobble forward on a bicycle. A shoulder-height evergreen hedge surrounded our yard except where a cement path from our porch to the sidewalk divided our yard in two. My guys were taking turns riding along the front sidewalk up and down our street, and then into our driveway before returning to the sidewalk paralleling the street out front, and back again. Aaron wasn't quite getting the hang of it yet, but Andrew stuck with him, sometimes riding to show him how, and then steadying the bike as Aaron pedaled and wobbled.

"Come on, guys. We're going to the store for a minute."

"Aw, Mom, do we have to? Now? It's Saturday."

"Yes, but I only have to buy one thing. We'll be right back." So they parked the bike in our garage and hopped in the car with me. We drove to the nearest grocery store, walked inside where I grabbed a single jar of ground nutmeg, nothing else, and were back home in twenty minutes.

As we turned the last corner leading to our quiet street, neighbors stood in groups in our yard, and the neighbor's across the street. I stared. Both yards were ravaged. Minutes earlier a drunk driver had lost control of his black sedan in front of our house and climbed the curb. After plowing a wide hole through our evergreen hedge, he bounced off our massive elm tree with enough force to ricochet completely across the street and climb to the highest part of our neighbor's yard where he crashed against their big tree, and stalled. His crumpled vehicle still rested there.

"Didn't you see him?" neighbors asked, eyes wide, as soon as I parked my car and we climbed out. "You must have heard the police sirens as they took him away. It happened just minutes ago, right where your sons were playing—right after you left," they said, pointing down the street in the other direction. Rutted tire tracks stood in mute proof of the devastation.

I didn't quit shaking for a long time. I gathered my sons close and hugged them hard, thankful that God had known trouble was coming and sent me a message that took us out of harm's way at the perfect time. Soon our home filled with the satisfying smells of baked custard. I'm sure that was the most delicious one I ever made.

In my next day's Bible reading, I read of single mom Hagar raising her son, Ishmael, alone, when she couldn't find water in the wilderness. Their water bottle had run dry and they were about to perish, when God sent a watching angel who showed her a well of water and saved their lives.

I didn't see our angel, but I'll never forget her presence: God sent a nutmeg angel wafting whiffs of tantalizing spice so wonderful that I had to bake fresh custard that very day for my boys and me, because He wanted to get us safely away from home before destruction came.

Touched by an Angel

John D. Millirons as told to Caroline B. Phillips

I WAS REARED ON A 150-acre farm in southwest Virginia; we grew or raised everything we could possibly need, from farm animals and vegetables to sorghum and broom corn. Once a year, after my mother had canned and stored all we needed, we took wheat and corn to the mill to be ground into flour, the broom corn to be made into brooms, and the extra produce to the store to sell.

In 1917 the method of transportation for this trip was a farm wagon pulled by a team of trusty oxen. I was only five years old, so my fifteen-year-old brother, Louis, and my twelve-year-old sister, Annie, were chosen for the trip. My oldest brother, Edgar, who was nineteen, my mother, and I remained at home for my dad was away surveying.

About two hours after the wagon rumbled out of our valley for the five-mile trip to Wytheville, a terrible storm came up that sent torrents of water over the falls, causing streams to overflow their banks and flood the entire area below our house.

Since we lived on a hill, many visitors, usually on horseback, would stop at the gate and holler "Hello" if they were dropping something off or needed to give us a message. On this very stormy day, while starting a fire in the cookstove for my mother, I heard a loud, clear "Hello" summoning us to the door.

I went out on the porch to see who it was—and saw no one. My mother asked me who it was and I told her no one was there. Then we heard it again: a distinct, not alarmed, "Hello." This time Edgar stuck his head out of the barn and asked my mother who it was. By this time she and I were on the front porch looking for the person again.

When Edgar joined us, he glanced down at the flooded valley and swollen stream and asked, "What is that?" Upon closer inspection, we realized that it was the tip end of the wagon bobbing in the water with the tongue rising and falling. The oxen were nowhere in sight, and my brother and sister were sitting on the end, helpless.

Edgar quickly got a rope, tied it to a tree, waded out, and tied it to the wagon; along that rope he was able to carry my sister and brother to safety. The oxen, gasping for breath, were cut loose and swam to shore.

The local paper reported the event and two preachers came to the house to discuss it with my mother, but no one ever came forward to say they were at our gate and no tracks of any kind were found in the soft mud. I will always believe we were called to the door by an angelic power that enabled us to save my family from great sadness.

The Midnight Traveler

Linda Howton as told to Joyce Gatton

MY JOB IN THE IT DEPARTMENT'S command center for a grocery distribution center required me to work the late shift. My workweek started on Sunday evenings. One particular November Sunday seemed no different from others. Because of the late hours we worked, we usually had a laidback atmosphere. I had a good camaraderie with my three male coworkers. When time came to pass the day's work to the oncoming shift, however, we were always glad to stand at the time clock and wait for the midnight hour to toll so we could head home.

Our cars were parked in front of the well-lit office, and the four of us always walked out together. On this cold November night my supervisor and I chatted as we walked to my car. We said good night, and he walked to his car a couple of parking spaces away while I opened my car door. I was happy to be getting into my new Chevy Lumina for my fifteen-mile trip home.

The interior light came on, and I glanced into the empty backseat as I slipped behind the steering wheel. Breathing in the cold November air, I backed out of the parking space and headed for home, thinking of my warm bed.

I pulled out from the frontage drive and onto the main street that ran north and south. My four car doors had automatically locked, so I felt safe enough driving home by myself on the same route I'd been using for twenty years. I headed north over the bridge that crossed the Kansas River, then rounded the curve on the exit ramp going west onto Kansas Highway 32.

Suddenly, when I made the turn onto the exit ramp, I felt the presence of a person in the car with me. I knew that couldn't be the case. My car was clearly empty when I unlocked it in the parking lot. However, the feeling of someone else's presence kept getting stronger and stronger. And stranger yet, I had a total absence of fear.

I continued heading west toward home, merging onto the divided highway. I saw no other cars, which was normal for the midnight ride home. The Kansas River and a set of railroad tracks ran parallel to me on my left, and a few closed businesses were on my right. A small bakery, car lot, grocery store, the post office, and a couple of bars were all dark. The tall streetlights illuminated the road and my car.

Finally, I was so overcome with the immediate presence of someone in the backseat that I turned to look. Sitting behind the passenger's seat was a young man who appeared to be in his early twenties. He smiled at me as if he were extremely happy to be in the car with me. He didn't say a word.

He had short brown hair and a perfectly trimmed brown beard. He was wearing a heavy, collared, long tweed coat, buttoned down the front. He looked immaculate. His hands seemed to rest in his lap, although I couldn't see them. I had to turn back around to watch the road in front of me; I was driving about fifty-five miles per hour. I noticed the dead grass in the median strip as I drove on. The businesses became fewer and fewer, and the homes along that stretch of the road sat back a long way from the highway.

I knew I wasn't in a dream. I was clearly aware of the scenery passing me. However, I was traveling with a man who could not possibly be mortal. My emotional state was one of elation.

There's a man in my car! There's a man in my car! There's a man in my car! I kept saying to myself.

It was as if I was singing the words to a song over and over. I turned around to look at him again. He still had that joyful smile on his face, and I felt incredible peace. In fact, I'd never felt such ultimate tranquility before. I was so overcome with the joy that appeared on his face that I didn't think about asking him who he was and why he had appeared to me. The longer I drove, the more the sense of peace, joy, and tranquility overpowered me.

A few minutes later I looked at the man again. He communicated to me, not with an audible voice but from his mind to my mind, *"I'm just going to ride with you for a little while."*

It was so amazing. Who would ever believe me? Surely no one in his or her right mind would. I continued to drive and turned to look at him again. The same joyful smile greeted me. The muscles in my face started to tire as I realized I had been smiling a huge smile ever since I felt his presence.

Because I was so astounded at his appearing and was filled with complete calm, the obvious need to ask why he was there simply didn't hit me. But I didn't need to ask in order to know he wasn't from Kansas.

The surrounding countryside became sparsely populated. Still several miles from home, I entered the small town of Edwardsville, with its one and only stop-light. When I stopped at the light, I suddenly knew the man was no longer in my car. The overwhelming peace of his presence left.

I had driven that path countless times at all different hours of the night. Never before or in the nine years after did anyone else appear. I can only speculate that God sent this man to protect me from a danger that night, from something I had no way of knowing was in my path.

At times when I start to doubt God's presence, He immediately draws me back to that night. Then I remember the man's face and the peace I felt. It brings me a renewed level of comfort each time I need it.

Hand of an Angel
Cindy Huron

ASKING MY SWEETHEART IF HE BELIEVED in divine intervention, I received the reply, "Oh yes," with conviction. This surprised me because Rich leans toward the skeptic concerning matters of spiritual nature. If he were convinced of an angel's interception, then I wanted to hear the story! It took place, he said, about thirty years ago, when he and his first wife, Kathy, were driving through Oregon.

"On our first night we stayed at a little motel near the Rogue River," Rich said, "and being a warm summer evening, we sat outside the cabin. A German couple from the cabin next door also sat outside. We noticed their distinctive accents and asked where they came from, and that started a pleasant evening of conversation.

"The next morning, Kathy and I packed up and drove north through the Cascade Range, hoping to visit Crater Lake, over seven thousand feet above sea level. As we approached the north entrance to the park, we heard on the radio that the park road was closed due to snow and thick fog. We couldn't believe our ears—it was June! Disappointed, we continued south toward Fort Klamath and discovered a southern entrance to the park that was still open. The ranger at the gate didn't charge us the entrance fee because, he said, we wouldn't be able to see anything through the fog.

"As we drove up the crater mountain, the fog grew thicker and thicker, with light snow falling, making visibility extremely poor. When we reached the parking lot, we crawled to a stop in front of a short stone wall. If you held your hand out, you could hardly see it, the fog was so thick. We knew the lake was somewhere behind the wall, so I stepped up onto the wall, thinking I would at least walk down to the lake's edge. At that moment, we heard another car drive into the parking lot and stop. A distinct voice with a German accent reached through the fog, so I stepped down from the wall and walked over with my wife to greet the couple we'd met the evening before. After chatting for a short while, we all felt chilled to the bone, and since the weather didn't improve, we climbed back into our cars and drove out of the park.

"The next year, my wife and I took our newborn son back to the same spot. It was a beautiful, clear summer day. We drove up the same southerly entrance route. I parked, facing the same stone wall, got out, and prepared to step onto the wall, as I had done the year before. But when I looked over, there was nothing, no foothold, no ledge, nothing except a thousand-foot drop. My knees suddenly went weak. I realized just how close I had come to dying the previous year.

"If it hadn't been for perfect timing, and for the distinct accent of our German friends, I would have stepped over that wall. My wife would be a young widow, and our son would never have been conceived. I was a split second away, virtually on the edge of death. I honestly believe that some angel—some divine hand of intervention—stepped in and pulled me back from that edge."

CHAPTER 6

Signs from Above

But your dead will live, Lord;

their bodies will rise —

let those who dwell in the dust

wake up and shout for joy —

your dew is like the dew of the morning;

the earth will give birth to her dead.

—Isaiah 26:19 (NIV)

Angels among Us
Gail Harris

MY BEST FRIEND'S HUSBAND CALLED with news I had been dreading. "Debbie's gone," Gary said. Her four-year battle with Hodgkin's disease was over.

Debbie and I had shared so much. We'd attended grammar and high school together in Massachusetts, been maids of honor at each other's weddings, and had children around the same time. We found humor in things other people never noticed. Her laugh was unforgettable. She had short blonde hair, sparkling blue eyes, and distinctive, angular features. Debbie always claimed she was average-looking. But she was beautiful to me.

I didn't know how I would go on without Debbie, but I had to be strong for her daughters, Stephanie, eight, and Jennifer, eleven. I flew to Massachusetts for the funeral. The day after, Gary, the girls, and I took a ride to one of Debbie's favorite places, a colonial plaza with candle shops and Christmas stores. I wanted to get the girls something that would remind them of their mom.

As we wandered through one of the shops, I spotted three wooden angels among the knickknacks. They had short blonde hair, blue eyes, and distinctive, angular features. "Look at these!" I exclaimed.

Jennifer gasped. "They look like Mom," she said, picking up the angel who had her hands clasped in prayer.

Stephanie liked the angel who was blowing a kiss. "After Mommy got her bone-marrow transplant she had to wear a mask and could only blow kisses," she said softly.

The final angel—one holding a present—was what Gary wanted. It reminded him of how generous Debbie had been.

At the register the cashier peered at our purchases. "Where did you find these?" she asked, frowning.

I pointed to the far aisle.

"These aren't in our inventory," she insisted, looking puzzled. She inspected the figures for price tags, but there weren't any. So she scoured the store for similar angels. She came back empty-handed.

"That's odd," she said, and ended up charging us a nominal price for all three.

As we walked out, the girls started giggling about their mystery finds. I heard Debbie in their laughter. Even more, though, I felt God helping us all to go on.

Rainbow Connection

Jane Martinec

PEPE WAS A BLACK CHIHUAHUA, but he had a personality the size of a Great Dane. When my dad called, "Here, boy," Pepe jumped into his lap or followed him anywhere. Pepe even waited outside the bathroom door while my dad shaved in the morning and again when he brushed his teeth before bed.

Whenever we visited Dad my children liked to play with Pepe and wind him up to the point where their grandpa called Pepe "wild."

"Have you tamed little Pepe yet?" my twins, Emily and Joey, loved to ask when they called Grandpa.

"Still wild," Grandpa would say.

When Dad passed away, Pepe came to live with us. He loved the kids. Pepe insisted on sitting perfectly in the middle of them whenever we got in the car—but sometimes I believed he missed Dad as much as I did.

Eventually Pepe's joints got stiff, and he lost his eyesight to cataracts. We decided it wasn't fair to keep Pepe alive any longer.

"Grandpa will be waiting for Pepe in heaven, just over the rainbow bridge," I reminded the kids when we got to the vet's office that fateful day. I could only pray that my story was true.

I held Pepe gently as the vet gave him the shot. Suddenly I heard my father's voice, just as clearly as if he were standing beside me. "Pepe!" Dad called. "Here, boy!" Pepe's head raised up off the vet's table and turned toward my father's voice. Then Pepe was gone. I could almost see him running into my father's arms, just over that rainbow bridge.

Under an Angel's Wings
Michelle W. F. Carll

I GAVE BIRTH TO A beautiful baby girl in the summer of 1994. My husband, Don, and I named her Lindsay. She appeared healthy, but when our daughter was nearly six weeks old, doctors told us she had a rare genetic kidney disease.

We went to a kidney specialist who gave us bleak statistics: 80 percent of children with this disease die in the first year. If Lindsay did survive, her kidneys would fail and a transplant would be necessary. She needed to be admitted to the hospital for treatment to prevent her body from retaining fluid and to get the nutrition she needed to grow. Don and I were stunned by the news and we prayed our baby would beat the odds.

The next several days were filled with surgeries and tests. All went well until one morning after Lindsay's bath. The monitors showed a drop in her heart rate and she was rushed to pediatric intensive care.

A few days later, after more tests, doctors approached us with devastating news. Lindsay had gone into kidney failure, which led to several massive strokes and left her severely debilitated. When they told us she was existing solely on life support, we knew there was no hope.

Almost two months from the day she was born, at about nine in the morning, doctors, nurses, and therapists gathered in Lindsay's room as the chaplain said a prayer. After life support was disconnected everyone left. My husband and I held Lindsay and rocked her gently. Around 9:45 AM Lindsay took her last breath.

In the days that followed, friends and family surrounded us with love and support. Among the many cards and letters, one in particular moved me. It was accompanied by a drawing and sent by Sharon Efird, a woman from our church choir.

"On September 8, at about 9:45 AM, I felt restless and could not keep my thoughts on my work," she wrote. "I stopped to look out the window to try to quiet my mind. I saw a distinct cloud of an angel with wings spread and sunlight bright from the face. It kept its shape for several minutes while I made this sketch. A great peace came over me as the shape faded. It wasn't until almost noon that I heard Lindsay had died. I have no doubt that she's in heaven."

When I saw Sharon a few days later, I told her how much her note meant to us. During our conversation I found out she didn't know the time of Lindsay's death. Then I felt sure—she had witnessed our little girl's welcome to heaven.

Life after Life
Caroline Updyke

THERE'S A REASON MY HUSBAND, Eric, and I got satellite radio. It's reliable. We live in a woodsy, hilly area, and just driving around town I used to lose my favorite station or the signal would get crossed with one from another station. That never happens with satellite radio. We have it set to an oldies channel. The signal is locked in, the sound crystal clear.

That day I was especially glad to have music to listen to, anything to take my mind off my terrible sense of loss.

My family and I had just left the nursing home where my grandmother—my beloved *abuela*—had lived the last years of her life. We had gone to visit her husband, Jim. He was ninety-four and quite frail.

When he dies, I thought, *there will be no more reason to come here, and my last connection to* Abuela *will slip away.*

I could feel myself starting to cry. As Eric pulled out of the parking lot, I reached for the volume knob and turned it up. I didn't want my eight-year-old twins, sitting in the back, to hear me.

I'd always thought that there'd be the comfort of knowing *Abuela*'s soul still lived on. That I'd feel some tangible assurance she was in heaven. But when she passed, there was nothing. Only an emptiness I couldn't fill.

We were such kindred spirits, *Abuela* and I, upbeat, full of energy, every day a reason to celebrate. The happiest I ever saw her was the day she married Jim. She was eighty-six then but as giddy as a teenager. It didn't matter to her that the marriage likely wouldn't be long. She was in love, and going to live every minute to the fullest.

Now she'd been gone for two months. One moment I'd been holding her hand, feeling her spirit still pulsing through her. The next instant it vanished. Was that it? Was that all? *Where did she go?*

If my *abuela*—so vital, so vibrant—could die and leave nothing of her spirit, then what was the point of believing? I felt like a part of me had died with her, the part that had faith God was with me.

"What's upsetting you the most?" Eric asked. He knew my grief went beyond missing my grandmother.

"I need to know that she went somewhere else. Where did she go, Eric?"

The satellite radio station was playing a Frank Sinatra song. We'd gone only several hundred feet when the music stopped suddenly. The signal cut out completely. A few seconds later the radio came back on. No Sinatra. No music at all. Just a voice saying, "There is life after life."

Then the signal faded again and our oldies channel came back on.

I turned to Eric. "What was that?"

"I think you know what that was," he said.

And who.

Buddy's Welcome Home
Wanda Rosseland

OUT WEST WE'VE GOT A SAYING: The best hired man a rancher can have is a good cow dog. My husband, Milton, and I definitely had that in Buddy. One morning I looked out the window and scanned the pasture for his black-and-white fur. Our Border collie–shepherd mix was semiretired these days, but whenever he could he slipped out to stand guard over the cows.

As a young dog Buddy was ever present. When Milton and I went out to move cows, Buddy rode along in the pickup. He wove behind the drags to keep the cattle in line on our way to the gate. During calving season he put the cows safe in the shed with a couple of sharp barks. Feeding time was easy, especially in winter, with Buddy planted by the feed troughs ready to spring into action if a cow got too close to the tractor. "You know what, Bud?" I told him at least once a day. "You're the best dog in the world."

Maybe I should have been more strict about keeping him indoors. Buddy still wanted to do his job but arthritis had slowed him down, and the cows were dangerous. But I knew how much he loved to work. *So where was he now?* Milton was out feeding the cows with his tractor. Cows crowded around him, ignoring all his efforts to move them away. Buddy obviously wasn't with Milton. I left the window and opened the door to call. "Buddy!"

But I found him right there, stretched out on the step. When I bent down to touch him he flinched. Our Buddy was hurt! "Milton!" I cried. Just as I called out, he came running around the corner.

"What happened?" he said, dropping to one knee.

"I don't know. I just found him."

Milton gently felt around Buddy's body. "I don't feel anything broken," he said. "It doesn't look to me like he got kicked."

I brought Buddy some beaten eggs and milk, but he turned his head away after a few laps. Milton and I dealt with hurt animals all the time. As ranchers we had a lot of experience identifying injuries and taking care of them. So when Bud's stomach started to swell, we knew all too well what had happened: Cows charge and butt with their heads to defend themselves if they feel cornered. Bud must have been mauled and tossed in the air. His internal organs would have gotten bruised when he slammed back down to the ground. Pressure from the swelling can be fatal. Years before, Milton had gotten hurt when four big, round hay bales fell off a semitruck and landed on top of him. The bales had not only broken several bones, but crushed his internal organs. Milton's stomach swelled up just like Buddy's was now. We spent a long, awful week waiting and praying for the swelling to go down.

I knew that Buddy might not be so lucky. We carried him down to the basement and settled him on a soft, fluffy rug. The heat from the coal furnace warmed the room, and the exposed pine rafters smelled sweet and fresh. Buddy lay stretched out on his side, lightly panting. Now we just had to wait. I sat beside him, petting his head. *God, please don't let Buddy die. He's the best dog in the world, as You know.*

I was no stranger to grief. I'd lost two infant sons to a genetic disorder just hours after they were born. I tried to picture the boys together in heaven with the angels, but I couldn't truly imagine it. I'd never get over such loss, but I always thought that picture might be the one thing that would give me closure.

I thought of all the fun my other children had with Buddy. He followed them everywhere, played fetch for hours, cuddled with them on cold nights. He kept me company around the house, walked with me to the barn and down to the mailbox. He was made to run in the sagebrush and chase rabbits, to work and play with the people he loved. He loved everything about life. How could he be dying? I prayed constantly, but Buddy still lay deathly still, his legs straight out, refusing to eat any food or water.

I stayed by Buddy's side the following days, even slipping downstairs in the middle of the night to see him. One afternoon while doing the dishes I asked God outright: *Why haven't You healed him?*

Words dropped into my mind, and I knew that they came from God. "*Wanda,*" He said, "*he is grievously injured. He cannot live.*"

Weeping, I went down to the basement. I sat down beside Buddy and pressed my hand on his warm back, trying to deny those words, but knowing I could not. "I'm so sorry you got hurt, Bud," I said. "You're the best dog in the world. The very best..."

"Mom!"

The sharp voice had come from somewhere above my head. It was the voice of a child, a young boy. It sounded so real, but how could it be? I jerked my head up to see where it had come from.

"Let him go," the voice insisted. "We want to play."

I looked up at the ceiling, searching for the source of that voice, but all I saw were the lengths of smooth pine planks that made up the rafters until—

The wood dissolved into a wavy stream and disappeared. In its place were the bright shining faces of two young boys. They grinned down on me and Buddy. Around them a big circular parapet made of stone came into view, like a tower in an ancient castle. But I recognized my boys immediately. My heart shouted out to them in joy. They were waiting for Buddy! They wanted to play with him! Above them hung the most beautiful blue sky I'd ever seen. A sky no doubt filled to overflowing with angels.

The vision began to fade as the boys' faces retreated behind a misty fog of gray, the stone tower becoming once again the pine rafters of the basement ceiling. But the vision would stay with me forever, clear in my mind and heart. The boys waited in heaven. I had seen them with my own eyes. It was time for Buddy to go. I bent down to give him a kiss. "It's okay, Bud," I said. "You can go now. You can go on and play."

Not long after, Buddy closed his eyes and died. Milton and I buried him on the side of the hill where he loved to lay and watch the cows. But I knew Buddy had found more beautiful fields than these, where he could run and play and be loved by two brothers who knew he was the best dog in this world. And the next.

The Promise
Nikki McFaul

THE FIRST TIME I SAW Gloria Marshall she was singing in the choir at Fairview Community Church. My six-year-old son, Colin, pointed her out. "Mommy, there's my Sunday school teacher," he said. She was a small-framed woman with wispy brown hair haloing her face. And when she sang her face purely glowed.

My husband, four children, and I were newcomers at the church, and ever since we'd joined, Colin had been raving about his teacher. I patted his hand, grateful he liked her, thankful my kids were able to have the kind of Christian experience that had been missing in my own childhood.

While my mother was a traditional Christian, my father was not. They were divorced, and I'd lived with my mother, brother, and sister in a little duplex in California. As the choir sang that Sunday morning, I recalled those days vividly, especially the year I was eight. That was when Mama got cancer. We had a picture of Jesus on our living room wall, and sometimes Mama would look at it and say that if she died Jesus would take her to heaven, where she would watch over us.

One night I awoke to find Mama bending over the double bed where all of us children were sleeping. I watched dreamlike as she kissed each of us. The next morning she was gone. She'd been taken to the hospital, where she died that same day. She was forty years old. I thought about what Mama had said, that she would go to heaven and watch over us. More than anything, I wanted assurance that it was true.

I went to live with my father. He didn't believe Mama was in heaven. He explained that her soul had gone to sleep. Period. With time and tutoring I came to believe as he did, that death was an ending, that there was no consciousness, just the mist of eternal slumber.

That's pretty much the idea I'd lived with all my life. Then a few years ago I found a deeper, personal relationship with Jesus Christ. Now I was trying to believe in God's beautiful promise of eternal life. But to be honest, it was difficult sometimes to put those deeply ingrained doubts behind me.

After the service at church that Sunday morning, I made a point to meet Colin's teacher. Gloria Marshall was a single parent with three children; she worked at a center for mentally handicapped children. As we talked, I had the compelling feeling that she was someone I should get to know better.

In the weeks to come, however, I saw her only occasionally at church functions. Then one December afternoon I plopped into a dining room chair to read the church newsletter. Inside was a note from Gloria thanking the church for supporting her as she faced a recurrence of her cancer. Cancer? Why, I didn't even know she was sick!

As I sat there, Tiger, our old tabby, slinked over and purred against my leg. I rubbed the cat's ear, a sudden idea nibbling in my thoughts. In my work as a stress counselor I often used positive mental imagery to help clients find healing. Maybe Gloria would consider working with me, no charge.

She was more than willing, and we began therapy sessions in January, meeting weekly in my office and at home. Gloria and I experimented with various meditations and visualizations that would help her envision God's love and healing being released into her life. Inviting a healing image into the mind can have a powerful effect on the body, and Gloria and I kept searching for the one just right for her.

One day as we began our session, a unique, imaginative image popped into my head. "Close your eyes, Gloria," I told her. "Call up a picture of a winged horse." As she followed my direction, I said, "Imagine that he has been sent to you by God and he can fly you anywhere you choose to go. Now climb upon his back and let him take you to your own special healing place."

Maybe it was whimsical, but after a few minutes, when Gloria opened her eyes she was more relaxed than I'd ever seen her. "Oh, Nikki," she cried, "he took me to the most beautiful garden, where I walked and talked with Christ. There were flowers and springs of water."

The winged-horse meditation became her favorite. Again and again she would travel to the imaginative garden to meet the reality of Christ's presence. During her communion she often pictured Jesus giving her "living water" from the springs along the garden paths.

As spring came and went, a bond of closeness formed between us. Best of all, Gloria improved. An exam showed her inoperable tumor was actually shrinking. "Whatever you're doing, keep doing it," her doctor said. And we did.

Meanwhile, Colin's attachment to Gloria deepened too. She became his most beloved babysitter. One weekend Gloria kept Colin so that my husband and I could get away for some time together. When we returned, Colin was quieter than usual. That night I tucked him in bed, planting a kiss on his forehead.

"Mommy, what will happen to Gloria if she dies?" he asked.

"Gloria will live in heaven with Jesus," I answered, hoping he did not sense the uncertainty in my voice.

Colin closed his eyes, but the little frown of worry remained on his face.

Gloria had been progressing for six months when the change began. Gradually I noticed her energy waning. She grew thinner. Soon the doctor confirmed my fear: the tumor was growing again.

Before long Gloria was unable to go on with our sessions. At our last one she presented me with a ceramic figure she'd made herself, a pastel blue horse. A winged horse.

"I will not give up hope, but I have to face the possibility I may die," she told me. "Perhaps the healing garden in my meditation is really heaven." She said it with such peaceful simplicity that I thought my heart would break.

"No!" I protested.

Gloria knew I struggled with doubts about the hereafter, and she interrupted me, a twinkling light in her eyes. "When I die, I'm going to be your best guardian angel, Nikki. I'll still be around. You'll see."

Autumn arrived. I threw myself into a busy schedule. I called Gloria often. Her voice seemed weak, like a sound fading in my ear. But while the leaves turned loose and drifted away, Gloria held on.

It was during the Christmas Eve service at church that I discovered her condition had suddenly worsened. After church I hurried to her house. Gloria's bed was surrounded with people speaking in hushed tones. "She's in a coma," her mother told me.

I lifted Gloria's hand into mine. "It's Nikki," I said. "I'm here. I love you." Her eyelids flickered. For a moment she seemed on the verge of speaking, then she lapsed back into her comatose sleep. I squeezed her hand and left. Outside, Christmas tree lights flickered in windows along the street. I knew I would not see Gloria again.

At home I retreated into my office, feeling desolate. Oddly, the pain of losing Gloria kept mingling with memories of my mother. I remembered that my mother had died at the same age Gloria was now, of the very same disease.

Oh, Gloria . . . I picked up the ceramic winged horse from my desk, thinking of the garden she had visited in her meditations. If only there could be a place like that!

Gloria died early Christmas morning. During the late afternoon, we attended her memorial service at the church. Gloria had requested we sing the French carol "Angels We Have Heard on High." But even when we sang the chorus, "Gloria in excelsis Deo," setting Gloria's name to angelic music, I could find little peace.

Later I stood before my bedroom window. The night was cold and starry. I gazed into the darkness for a long while, then went to bed, exhausted.

In the wee hours of the morning I awoke from a deep sleep, strangely alert. I cannot begin to explain what happened next. I simply felt what I thought to be the cat sink onto the foot of the bed against my feet. Tiger knew good and well she was not allowed on the bed. I moved my foot to nudge her to the floor, but she was not there. Then I remembered . . . I had put Tiger outside for the night.

I peered through the shadows. There was nothing on my bed at all, but the weight remained! It pressed against my feet, unmistakably, gently.

Suddenly a peculiar warmth glowed in the room as if it were enveloped by an electric blanket. My friend Gloria was there. I knew it. The certainty of it seemed indisputable to me.

I do not know how long I lay there with the mysterious pressure on the foot of my bed, but I had the overwhelming feeling that any moment I might actually see her sitting there.

Gradually, though, the weight on the bed disappeared. As it did, my mind was seized by a mental picture, like a movie playing on a screen inside my head. I saw Gloria in white, walking through a garden of unspeakable beauty, a garden blooming with bright flowers and flowing with streams of silver water. I saw her reach out her hand to a shining figure who I knew was Christ.

The image faded. I drifted into tranquil sleep.

When the alarm buzzed some hours later, the room was harsh with sunlight. I climbed from the bed, trying to come to grips with the experience of the night before. In the cold light of day, my intellect wanted a rational explanation. How could such a thing have happened? Was it some imagined illusion? Or had Gloria actually reached across the gulf to give me the assurance I needed so desperately in my life?

Bewildered, I wandered into the hallway. There I bumped into Colin, hurrying from his bedroom. His face was lit with wonder, with that special look a child gets when he sees something wonderful for the very first time.

"Mommy," he said, "why was Gloria sitting on my bed last night smiling at me?"

I gazed into his small upturned face, transfixed. Precisely at that moment I remembered Gloria's words: "When I die, I am going to be your best guardian angel. I'll still be around. You'll see."

I took Colin in my arms. "Perhaps Gloria came to assure you she is fine," I said full of certainty.

Today, two years after Gloria died, I still marvel at the glimpse of another reality that God granted to Colin and me that Christmas. I don't know why it happened. I only know I found the assurance I had longed for all my life—that death is merely a portal into another dimension, a heavenly dimension, which like the garden in Gloria's meditation brims with beauty and life and the radiant presence of Christ.

Seeing Only What's Really There

Rhoda Blecker

ONE OF MY GRANDSONS IS AUTISTIC. Kevin's autism manifests itself in a very specific way: he can reproduce perfectly, in painting or in sculpture, anything he can actually see. I have a picture of him at the age of three, standing in front of an easel, painting the vase of flowers on the table in front of him, and his talent has only grown over the years.

However, he cannot make an image of anything that isn't concrete, solid. His mind does not let him imagine. His mother, Linda, tells me that in all the years she has taken care of him—he is presently in his twenties—he has never been able to talk to her about anything that does not have a real existence.

The family, which lives hundreds of miles away, came to visit me about a month after my husband, Keith, died. They were unable to come sooner because Frank, my husband's "son," had just started a new job and was not able to get compassionate leave. Keith had raised Frank, but there had never been a legal adoption. We considered Frank and Linda's children our grandchildren, and they called us "Grampa Keith" and "Grama Ro."

By the time they arrived, the funeral was long over, and I was trying to cope. They stayed for a week, then went back to their home in Northern California.

Linda and I talked on the phone often, but it wasn't until just about six weeks ago that we had a conversation that flabbergasted me.

I told Linda that I loved being in Keith's and my home, that coming back to it after shopping, or after teaching one of my classes at the local community college, or after a contentious visit to Social Security or the lawyer's office always seemed somehow like an embrace.

"Well, of course it does," Linda said. "Kev told me after we got home last September that while we were visiting you, he saw Grampa Keith in the house."

I was speechless.

Linda went on, "We don't know how an autistic's brain works. They see the world in an entirely different way from us."

After we hung up, I sat still in the living room and tried to process what she had told me. Kevin could not imagine anything—and he had seen Keith here in the house. I felt as if God had sent Kevin to reassure me that I was not alone, that my beloved was still here, with me. It was a message that I would have dismissed from anyone else, but that I could not disbelieve, because it came from the perfect messenger.

The Music Box
Shirley Miller

MY HOBBY IS COLLECTING MUSIC BOXES—nothing expensive or rare or old, just music boxes I like and enjoy listening to. For years my mother's favorite was a figurine of an old woman sitting in a rocking chair and holding a few balloons.

Every time my mother came to visit me, she would go into the den and look at the music box and smile thoughtfully. Then she'd say, "If Pa goes first, that's me—sitting on a rocking chair in Lincoln Park, selling balloons." We would laugh. Then she would push the button and listen to the song it played—"Try to Remember" from the Fantasticks.

In 1970, Mother, then approaching eighty, suffered a mild stroke that put her in the hospital for a week. After that, she never became completely well again. Gradually her weakness increased. My father, who had been retired for several years, now became Mother's constant attendant. My sister and I took turns going over there one day a week to shop, clean house, and prepare casseroles and stews that my father could warm up for their meals.

Often my mother would ask me, "How's the old lady with the balloons?"

"Fine," I'd say. "She asks about you all the time." And we'd laugh.

In October 1974, my phone rang very early one morning. It was my father. He said, "Honey, you'd better get over here. It's Ma."

"What happened?" I asked, fearing the worst.

"She fell getting out of bed," he said. "I don't have the strength to lift her."

"I'll be right there," I said. I called my sister, told her the bad news, and said I'd pick her up on the way.

We found Mother sitting on the floor in her room, resting against her bed. Her face was sad and helpless, with tears of humiliation in her eyes. We got her back in bed.

"I'm sorry this happened," she whispered. "Thanks for coming. I'll make it up to you."

Those were her last words to us.

I called the doctor. An ambulance was there in minutes, but on the way to the hospital Mother lost consciousness. She was put into intensive care; while out in the waiting room the doctor told us, "It's very bad. There's been a lot of brain damage. She may not come out of this."

It was the beginning of a long ordeal for all of us. Mother went into a coma. Ten days later she was transferred to a private room where we could stay with her all day. Dad left the room frequently for a cigarette, his pain a constant frown on his face.

I was there every day, all day. Mother remained in a coma but I talked to her anyway hoping she could somehow hear me. "We're all praying for you, Ma," I told her, "everybody—even the old lady with the balloons."

Early in the morning on November 19, with our house still in darkness, the phone rang. I braced myself. "Hello?"

"Mrs. Miller, this is the head nurse at the hospital. I'm sorry to have to tell you that your mother died ten minutes ago."

Even though I had been expecting them, her words were like a blow. "Thank you," I managed to say somehow. "I'll take care of everything." As I hung up, I glanced at the clock. It was 5:10 AM. My mother had died at 5:00 AM, after being in a coma for forty-nine days.

Somehow we all got through the next few days. Then came the strain of adjusting to the loss, of waiting for the sorrow to fade. Time passed, but the sorrow did not disappear. When death takes a loved one, even though you trust in the promise of everlasting life, something in you longs for reassurance, for proof of that promise. It's only human, I guess.

The months went by. One season slipped into another. One day, my husband, Lenny, came home from work with a bad cold. I suggested that he spend a couple of days in bed, but he said he had too much work to do at the office and couldn't spare the time. A few days later, the cold was so bad that he had no choice. I nursed him all day, and then, so he could sleep undisturbed, I spent the night on the sofa in the den.

It had been a hard day for me, because it was the day before the first anniversary of Mother's death. I kept thinking about her, missing her, wishing she were only a telephone call away. It would have been so helpful just to talk to her, ask her advice about Lenny, feel the warmth and reassurance she always gave.

Tired and worried about Lenny, I tossed fitfully on the sofa for a while. I kept thinking about all the uncertainties of life, and I felt lost and lonely somehow. I missed our familiar bed and Lenny's comforting presence. Finally I drifted off into a restless sleep.

Hours later I woke with a start; something strange, something unfamiliar had wakened me. For a moment I didn't know what it was. Then I heard the music. The soft sounds of a familiar song drifted through my mind. But where was it coming from? There was darkness all around me. Had I been dreaming it? No, the music was still playing. In the darkness I could still hear its eerie tinkling.

I sat up. I stared into the gloom. There, on the desk, was the silhouette of the old lady with the balloons, and the song I heard coming from the music box was my mother's favorite, "Try to Remember."

"But it can't be playing," I said to myself. "Nobody's touched it. And the last time I played that box I distinctly remember letting it run down!"

And then I remembered what day it was. November 19. I glanced at the desk clock. It was 5:00 AM. Ma had died exactly one year ago to the day, to the hour, to the minute! I began to cry. I whispered to the dark: "If that's you, Ma, I hope you're safe and happy. You know that we still love you and miss you and, yes, we still remember."

I lay down again, weeping, listening to the music until it stopped, and I fell asleep, reassured at last.

I awoke again around 7:30 AM and smelled bacon. I got up and went to the kitchen. There was Lenny, shaved, fully dressed, at the stove frying bacon and eggs. "You were so sound asleep that I decided to fix breakfast myself," he said. "I'm going to work."

I stared at him, astonished. "Are you well enough for that?"

"Yes," he said. "During the night the cold just seemed to melt out of me. I feel great."

I felt as if I were going to cry again. "I'll do that," I said. I took the spatula away from Lenny and turned my back to him, close to tears.

Lenny went to the table and sat down to his cup of coffee. He said, "Tell me something. Did I hear you playing Ma's music box during the night or did I dream it?"

I fought the tears. I couldn't talk about it yet.

"No," I said. "I didn't play it."

And in my heart I thanked the Lord for using a little mechanical music box to let us know that our mother was safe with Him, that she still loved us, still missed us, and, yes, still remembered.

Encounter in the Gazebo
Brenda Vickers

RENARD WAS MORE THAN A DOG. He was the brightest spot in my life. In our fifteen years together, he'd made me a happier person. Even my husband, Jerry, said so. I smiled more, I laughed louder. So how was I going to face the days ahead without him? The kitchen was so quiet as I made dinner. No sound of Renard's nails clicking on the floor. No snowy white face smiling up at me as I cooked. No feathery white tail wagging when I smiled back. I'd had other canine companions in my life, but to me that pure white American Eskimo dog was more like an angel than a dog.

When Jerry got home from work, we picked at some leftovers. Neither of us was hungry. We barely spoke, both afraid that once we let our feelings out we wouldn't be able to stop. "Renard was very sick," Jerry said finally. "We should be happy he's in a better place."

"I know we should," I said. "But I can't. Not yet."

If only I knew for sure Renard was really safe in heaven, maybe I could let go. But right now all I felt was the loss. I got up to clear the table. Everywhere I looked I saw signs of Renard: his food dish and water bowl in the corner by the kitchen window, the cool bathroom tile where he always liked to lie, the calendar beside my bed that reminded me his birthday was *tomorrow*. I considered going for a walk just to get out of the house, but what good would that do? The yard was filled with reminders of Renard too: the gazebo where we used to sit and watch the birds at the feeder, the grass where he rolled around and played, the spot in the driveway where he liked to nap. *God, it would help so much to know that Renard is at peace with You.*

I tried to watch some TV with Jerry, but I couldn't keep my mind on the show. "I'm going to call it a day," I said. "Don't stay up too late." I went back to the kitchen for a glass of water. A strange noise made me stop at the window. I listened. Was it honking? It sounded like it was coming from the driveway, but the "honk" was like no car I'd ever heard. I had to see what it was.

The night was unseasonably warm when I stepped out the kitchen door. A white form stood out in the darkness. Something was resting in Renard's napping spot. I blinked hard, thinking my eyes must be playing tricks. But no. As I moved closer I saw that there was something there. An animal, in fact. But not a dog—a goose. A snowy white goose.

The little bird honked in the most distressed way. He was desperate to get somebody's attention. Where had he come from? There were no farms nearby. Nobody who kept geese. He had to be wild, but what kind of wild goose looked as pristine as this?

I stepped forward slowly, not wanting to scare him. Instead of backing away the goose marched over to me. He went past me into the backyard, looking over his shoulder as if he wanted me to follow.

So I did. *Where is his flock? Where is his mate? What does he want?*

The goose walked until he came to our gazebo and sat down in the grass. I ran into the house, filled Renard's dog dish with birdseed, and brought it out with some fresh water. The goose bent down his long neck and sipped at the water. Then he stood up and reseated himself in the water dish.

I couldn't help but laugh, he fit the bowl so snugly. He seemed to agree. He got up a moment later and shook himself, throwing me a look that seemed to say, *"Do you have anything in a larger size?"*

I had no intention of leaving this show. I sat down on the grass. "Where did you come from?" I asked. The goose cocked his head before making a chirping sound, as if considering the question before answering. I didn't understand his answer, not speaking goose myself, but I couldn't resist asking more. "Where are you going? Do you like the gazebo?" The goose answered each question with the same serious chirp. It reminded me of the way Renard used to listen when I spoke, how we understood each other without words. When I looked at my watch I couldn't believe how much time had passed while I sat with this funny little goose. "I'd really better go now," I said when the goose blinked his eyes sleepily.

I got up and started to the house. To my surprise the goose ran after me, honking. "What's going on?" asked Jerry at the kitchen door.

I introduced him to my new friend. "We had a long chat, but he's still got more to say . . ." The goose honked for a few more minutes. When he was finished, he marched away. I expected him to wander out of the yard, maybe even fly off. Instead he curled up in the driveway in the very same spot I'd found him—Renard's napping place. From a distance those white feathers looked exactly like Renard's white fur. I could almost believe it was Renard sleeping there peacefully. It wasn't just that he looked like Renard. It was that for the first time since Renard's death something was making me smile.

I kept that picture in my mind when I got into bed. In fact I got up several times to check on my mysterious visitor. Each time I looked he was right where I'd left him, curled up in his soft feather circle. At around 6:00 AM I awoke to his honking. The honks got fainter and fainter, and I knew my evening visitor was taking his leave.

I glanced at the calendar beside my bed, a red heart marking Renard's birthday. What more could I wish for him than perfect peace with God and the angels in heaven? A white-winged visitor had assured me that my angel Renard was curled up on a cloud in the best place any of us could ever imagine.

A Mother's Love

B. J. Taylor

I SAT AT MY DESK, looking out the window into my backyard. In forty-five minutes I'd be on my first live radio show. My stomach did flip-flops while I kept jiggling my legs, one crossed over the other.

The list of questions and my possible responses were laid out in front of me. *You're prepared. You can do this,* I thought. But I'd never been interviewed on a radio show before. Nagging doubts lingered: what if I messed up, said the wrong thing, made a fool of myself? This would be live, no margin for error. No taping and then editing out what didn't turn out right.

Many years ago, I won a writing award. The first person I called was my mother. She told everyone in her apartment complex about her daughter in California who now wrote for a magazine they all loved. She had a subscription, of course, and in each issue where I had a story appear she smiled happily and showed the story to her bridge and dominos partners, along with the folks making puzzles in the bright and airy craft room.

Our weekly phone chats were the best of times. We shared everything from everyday events like what she was making for dinner to talk about new stories I had written and the new rescue dog my husband and I had added to our life. His name was Charlie Bear. He was found running around on the streets in Los

Angeles and was rescued and then fostered before coming to live with me, my husband, and our mature golden Lab, Rex. Charlie Bear, a cute little munchkin, whom we later found out was a Havanese, came with some behavior problems, and in the beginning, my husband and I weren't sure we would be able to keep him. He threw temper tantrums, was sensitive to touch, and ferociously guarded his food. It was a learning curve for all three of us, well, four if you include Rex.

Phone calls with Mom were a great way to unwind from the stress. We'd always had dogs and cats romping through the house when I grew up so Mom was used to a new addition to the household and could offer advice. But nothing could have prepared us for Charlie Bear's problems.

"How's Charlie Bear adjusting?" she'd ask.

"Okay, I guess, but he has some issues."

"Don't we all?" she said and then laughed.

I loved the sound of her giggles and the way she told a funny joke, getting the punch line just right. Her cards and letters always contained a smiley face penned at the bottom and her loving and warm hugs were as close as a memory. It's what kept me going through the long months between visits from my home in California to Wisconsin where she lived and bolstered me through the constant tension of watching Charlie Bear as he adjusted to life under our roof.

Five days before Christmas in 2010, Mom passed away from complications of pneumonia. She'd been ill for so very long, and this wasn't unexpected, but my biggest fan, my biggest supporter, my biggest confidante was gone.

The following year, I decided to write a book about headstrong Charlie Bear, encouraging people to give rescue dogs a chance. Even though he came with issues, we worked them out. Mom would have loved that I wrote about it and would have enjoyed showing the book around on each of the three floors of her apartment complex. I could almost hear her exclaim, "Look at this, my daughter wrote a book!" But that was not to be.

For days I'd been preparing for the radio show. The host had sent me a list of possible questions, including what life lesson I've learned from a parent (that was easy: support, encourage, and love others), from my children (how to embrace life and live it to the fullest), and even how I want to be remembered (as someone who cares about people and animals alike). I wrote down some answers to other questions, as well, and spread them out on my desk, but my stomach was tumbling. Would I say the right things?

The phone rang. I glanced at the clock. It was still forty-five minutes before the show. I picked up the phone, pushed the talk button, and said, "Hello?"

No one was there.

"*Hmm*, that's odd," I mumbled, then looked at the handset. The caller ID read VIRGINIA.

That was my mom's name.

My biggest fan let me know she was in my corner. I breathed a huge sigh and then whispered, "*Thank you, Mom.*" I was ready now for that radio show.

Ushered into Heaven

He was taken up before their very eyes, and a cloud hid him

from their sight. They were looking intently up into

the sky as he was going, when suddenly two men

dressed in white stood beside them.

—ACTS 1:9–10 (NIV)

The Lady of the Light
Ned Dougherty

FAR, FAR AWAY IN THE DISTANCE, I thought I could hear voices. I struggled and strained to listen, to make contact. I was still immersed in total darkness, in a dark and heavy void. I began to float up, slowly but surely, drawn to the sounds that were still in the distance....

"I have no vitals! We're losing him!"

I was startled when I heard those words. I tried to lift my head up to see what all the commotion was about. I was flat on my back in some ambulance. I felt my face fall off to my left side and come to rest on my shoulder as I lifted myself up to focus on an emergency medical technician who was sitting at my side. I was facing the EMT, but when I tried to tell him that everything was okay, he didn't seem to hear or notice me. He was looking right through me as if I wasn't even there.

There was a lot of commotion at this point, which I didn't understand. I was sitting up and felt fine, but the driver was accelerating the ambulance while talking into a two-way radio. He was announcing to the hospital that the patient had just "coded." I heard my friend Bill shouting. "No, don't give up! You've got to make it! Hold on! Please, God, no!"

Instinctively, I looked down at the gurney. The EMTs were working feverishly on a patient who appeared to be dead. Then I realized that the patient on the gurney was me.

I felt the ambulance slow down as the driver braked to execute a turn at a fork in the road. But as the ambulance proceeded forward and accelerated rapidly, I found myself catapulted through the roof and suspended in midair, watching the ambulance move rapidly down the dark wooded roadway, lights flashing, into the distance.

It took me several seconds to understand this new predicament. I was hovering in midair, suspended maybe forty or fifty feet above the road. I realized something was missing—my body.

I looked down the dark road again. The ambulance was long gone now and along with it my body.

My attention was drawn to a brilliant, starlit sky. I confidently gazed at a particular grouping of stars and instinctively but inexplicably thought, *I'm going home!*

As a massive field of energy began to form in the sky directly in front of me, I heard a loud, grinding mechanical noise as the mass of energy shaped itself into a cylinder funneling upward. It seemed as if the darkness of the sky turned into liquid as the mass of energy curled like an ocean wave and formed a perfect tunnel that stretched into the heavens.

As I stared into the large and imposing tunnel of energy, a shimmering, luminescent-blue field of energy began to float down the tunnel toward me. As it rapidly approached, I watched the luminescent-blue field mass into a form and begin to materialize into an image of a human being. As the image composed itself, I found myself face-to-face with an old friend. His name was Dan McCampbell, but I had never expected to see him again. After all, he had been killed in Vietnam.

"Dan, I recognize you! What are you doing here?"

"Relax, everything is okay!" Dan communicated to me with his engaging smile. "I'm here to show you the way!"

Dan appeared to be young and very healthy, but his body was lighter, more ethereal than a human body. He appeared to be wearing combat fatigues that he would have worn in Vietnam.

As Dan and I communicated, I realized that we did not speak to each other as we had communicated in our earthly lives. We were communicating telepathically, which connotes a communication of words between minds by means other than by *vocal* communication, but such a description falls short of the spiritual communication we were experiencing. We were not only communicating with words; we were communicating with feelings and emotions. As we thought, we also emoted our thoughts. Both thoughts and emotions were being communicated telepathically and spiritually in a manner that far surpassed normal human communication.

Dan communicated to me, "You are on the threshold of an important journey. Each of these places and *events* that are before you are for you to absorb as much as you can. It is important that you remember *everything* that you see before you. You will be going back, and you must go back with what you experience. You have a mission ahead of you in your life, and this experience will guide you on that mission."

Dan led me toward the tunnel, and his presence was to my left as we moved forward.

I realized that I was comfortable with the fact that I had an ethereal human form but not a material body. I recognized that my being was in a natural state of existence, free of the limitations of the human body. I did not miss my human body and realized what a hindrance it was to be imprisoned in one.

As we entered the tunnel of energy, I heard, very sharply and clearly, the melodious sound of chimes and crystals and other wonderful—but unearthly—sounds. I focused my attention on the composition of the walls of the tunnel as we moved forward. They resembled a massive ocean wave in a tubular form.

I turned back to Dan and communicated my wonderment at what I was experiencing. If I had to communicate my thoughts by words, I would have been speechless. I communicated that thought also and Dan understood. I was experiencing the ineffable.

We exited the tunnel and were suspended in a universe of bright stars. We were moving like angels without wings. Dan was still guiding me. I looked back and noticed that the tunnel of energy was no longer visible. Instead, I was looking deep into a void of space. I knew Earth was in the direction from which we had come, but the planet was now just a speck of light among a million stars.

I turned back to ask Dan if we had really traveled so far that Earth was no longer identifiable, but he was no longer at my side.

Suddenly, I found myself standing in a beautiful garden setting. As I marveled at this incredible setting of nature, a brilliant light appeared in the garden. I found myself in the presence of a beautiful, radiant, angelic being, dressed in white with a veil that covered her head and flowed to the bottom of her full-length gown. A lighter veil covered her face, which was not fully visible. The light that radiated from her was of a heavenly brilliance that prevented me from fully observing her, but she was beautiful.

She became known to me as the Lady of Light. She began to communicate with me. Her manner was eloquent and soft-spoken, yet the tone of her message was serious. The Lady of Light waved her right arm, and I watched as scenes, as if in a movie, developed before me. I became aware that I was watching future events of my life, scenes that were incongruent with the life that I had been living so far.

The Lady of Light showed me scenes where I was writing manuscripts, researching materials and books, and embarking on a lifelong quest for truth and knowledge. The Lady of Light told me that I would begin by writing a book about my experiences and that my book would become a source of inspiration for many people in search of their true spiritual nature. The Lady of Light showed me that I would become involved in research in college and university settings. I was shown a future scene in a university auditorium in which I was conducting a seminar.

As I watched myself speaking from the stage in this future scene, I stood to the side of the auditorium with the Lady of Light. I watched as I was apparently addressing an audience of doctors, medical researchers, and students. As I absorbed this scene, I thought the Lady of Light must have had me confused.

"It is time for you to go back."

I started to protest. I wasn't ready to go back. I had too many questions. There was too much to be learned. I realized that my journey was about to end, but I wanted it to last forever. I felt the warmth and vibrancy of God's light pulsing through my being. I was without pain or suffering, which I had left behind in my human body.

Yet, I also now felt that God's light was preparing me—anesthetizing me—for my return to my body. It was time for me to reenter my body and return to my earthly existence. As I drifted backward, the brilliant light began to fade; the warm and loving glow that filled my being turned to darkness.

As I found myself reunited with my flesh, a painful jolt of electricity exploded in my chest. Suddenly, it was incredibly cold, and I was in darkness. I realized I was back in my body.

"We got him this time!" the paramedic exclaimed.

I had been successfully resuscitated. The EMTs sighed in relief as my vital signs were restored. They had brought me back. I should have had the greatest appreciation for their efforts, yet I didn't because I didn't want to be there!

Escort to Heaven

Radona Edgar

I PULLED INTO THE HOSPITAL parking lot while it was still dark. Four o'clock in the morning, when the halls were quiet, the lobby was empty, and only a skeleton staff manned the ward. That was how I preferred to see my older brother Marshall. It felt as if there was no one around but just the two of us. Too early for visiting hours, but the nurses wouldn't stop me. They knew Marshall's time was short.

My brother was always the one who could make me laugh, cheer me up when I was sad. Now, at age forty-nine, he was on a ventilator, drifting in and out of consciousness, suffering from multiple afflictions. I took a deep breath as I strode across the lot to the hospital doors, wondering if this would be my last visit with my brother. *No, God. I'm not ready.*

For forty-one days I'd headed straight to Marshall's room without seeing or speaking to anyone. This morning, however, a man sat in the lobby. He gave me a look like he'd been waiting for me. The very air in the room seemed to push me toward the stranger. "Good morning, ma'am," he said. "Have a blessed day."

I nodded and moved past the man down the corridor. At Marshall's bedside, the brief encounter sparked something in me. I said words I never thought I'd say to my brother. "Today is the day. Your angel is waiting in the lobby to escort you home."

I couldn't know why the stranger had been there, or where he had gone by the time I passed through the empty lobby on my way out. But when Marshall passed away that evening, I was finally ready to let him go. I knew my brother wasn't making the journey to heaven alone.

A Glimpse of Eternity

Catherine Marshall

"FACTS ARE OFTEN STRANGER THAN FICTION," people say. True. Still, many are going to find the facts of Betty Malz's story difficult to believe.

It's a story I can vouch for. Last October, in the living room of our Virginia farm, I heard this extraordinary adventure from Betty's own lips. Through subsequent weeks I investigated the details in depth. But that day at the farm I knew that the best and final proof was Betty Malz herself, along with her nine-year-old daughter, April Dawn (born after her mother's "death")—both so vibrantly alive.

The adventure began one June night in 1959. Betty, twenty-nine; her husband, John, a salesman for the Sun Oil Company in Indiana; their daughter Brenda; Betty's parents, the Glenn Perkinses; and her little brother had just arrived for a two-week family vacation at Gulf Vista Retreat, Florida. They spent that first day swimming, water-skiing, surfing, shell-hunting. Exhausted, Betty and her husband went to bed early.

Then the pain began. Hand pressed on her stomach, Betty Malz first wondered, *What did I eat for dinner?* Then as the pain increased, she thought, *What a way to start our vacation!* Finally Betty turned on the light and woke her husband. When the pain became excruciating, he drove her to the hospital.

Betty lay in the hospital several days while the doctors made dozens of tests and debated her situation. Finally she was sent by plane to a hospital in her hometown of Terre Haute, Indiana, where on the eleventh day of her illness, she was operated on by a gynecologist-surgeon. He found an appendix long-ruptured, with a huge mass of gangrene in her abdomen. Every organ was coated.

"I can give you no hope," the surgeon told her husband and her parents. "I've lost two-hundred-pound men in forty-eight hours with a fraction of the gangrene we have here. She can live only a few hours."

But Betty did not die that night, nor the next. In fact, on the fourth day she lapsed into a coma. She was to be in that coma for most of the next month.

The days passed. Ten. Twenty. Betty was given multiple blood transfusions (she had B-negative blood) and intravenous feedings. Not a mouthful of food passed her lips. Meanwhile, two more operations followed.

Betty's husband took time off from his business to maintain a constant vigil in her room—checking reports, seeking every possible avenue of hope. Her father, a clergyman, stood by her bed every day, his voice raised in praise and worship of the Lord.

More days passed—twenty-five, thirty. The doctors were certain that the comatose patient could see or hear nothing.

"That was not the case," Betty Malz told me during our interview. "All that time that I was a prisoner of my own body, when I couldn't speak, see, or smell, or control the movement of a muscle, I could hear everything the doctors, nurses, and visitors said. It was as though when my physical senses went, all spiritual senses were sharpened. If people came into my room feeling hopeless about me, I knew it. When they had faith that I would get well, I knew that, and it helped me. If only people could realize," Betty said with great emphasis, "that in any form of unconsciousness or coma—even under anesthetics, I do believe—unerringly the spirit picks up those attitudes."

Betty described how one day she heard footsteps coming into her room, followed by the pages of a book being turned. When the person quietly began to read a psalm, she recognized the voice of Art, a man she had never liked.

"In those days," Betty told me, "I was a thoroughgoing snob, and God chose this man as His instrument to correct that."

As Art read on—Psalm 107, all of it, and then Psalm 108—the words seemed to the helpless woman on the bed to be the most beautiful words she had ever heard: "Their soul abhorreth all manner of meat; and they draw near unto the gates of death. Then they cry unto the Lord in their trouble, and he saveth them out of their distresses. He sent his word, and healed them, and delivered them from their destructions" (Psalm 107:18–20, KJV).

"He sent his word and healed them." To the desperately ill Betty the words seemed written in fire. She had been handed her lifeline. Betty silently blessed the man whom she had despised.

Then came a new crisis. All supplies of B-negative blood in Terre Haute, Indianapolis, and St. Louis had been used. The doctor warned that unless they could find blood plasma for her immediately, Betty would be gone in a few hours.

Was it a coincidence that that very morning Betty's uncle Jesse, a freight conductor-dispatcher for the Pennsylvania Railroad, felt a strange inner prompting that he should leave his job and go immediately to offer his blood? Unacquainted with this kind of guidance, the man argued with the inner Voice. "This doesn't make sense. I'm at the end of a run, still miles from home. I don't want to go in my work clothes. I'll wait until late this afternoon after I'm cleaned up. Why, I don't even know if my blood is the right type."

But finding no inner peace, the conductor finally dropped what he was doing and headed for the hospital. They discovered that Uncle Jesse had B-negative blood. Once again the blood transfusion helped Betty rally.

On July 31, Betty's fever shot still higher as pneumonia set in. Then her veins collapsed completely; no more transfusions or intravenous feedings were possible.

"The battle is lost," the exhausted family was told. "You'd better get some rest. We'll call you if there's any change."

Sadly Betty's husband drove home and her parents drove the thirty-one miles to their home in Clay City.

At two thirty the next morning, Betty's father was sharply awakened—he did not know how. He had a strong compulsion to get to the hospital immediately. He resisted at first. Finally he gave in, dressed, and was on his way shortly after 4:00 AM.

Sometime after he had left the house, the telephone rang. It was a nurse calling. "Mrs. Perkins, I'm so sorry to have to give you this message. Your daughter Betty expired a few minutes ago." There was a pause. "I've already called her husband, of course. He will be coming over as soon as possible this morning."

Concern for her own husband temporarily overcame Mrs. Perkins's anguished grief. "But my husband is already on his way there. Please have someone watch for him and intercept him. It would be a dreadful shock for him to walk into Betty's room and find her."

The nurse promised—and hung up.

But Betty's father parked at the side of the hospital and slipped in through a nurses' exit door. This next part of the story I heard from Betty's father himself.

"I walked down the hospital corridor. Everything seemed too quiet, too deserted," he told me. "I remember how my heart skipped a beat as I rounded the corner . . . stood in the doorway . . . saw the still form on the bed. Betty was covered with a sheet. Every bit of apparatus had been removed, all instruments; even the chart was gone.

"I was stunned and despairing. I couldn't even pray. I could only stand by the bed softly crying, 'Jesus! Jesus!'"

How could the sorrowing man possibly have known the extraordinary adventure his daughter was experiencing at that moment? Let Betty tell it:

"I was walking up a steep hill. Yet there was no muscular exertion, it was more like a light skipping or floating movement, without effort. I thought, *Why, steep hills have always affected the muscles in the calves of my legs.* There was none of that—all movement was a delight. The grass under my feet was a vivid green and of a velvety texture, yet every blade seemed alive.

"To my right was a high silvery marble wall. To the left, slightly behind me, was a tall angel. I could see only his feet as he walked, and the bottom of his garment swaying as in a gentle breeze. In the near distance were the echoes of multitudes of voices singing, worshiping Jesus.

"As the angel and I reached the top of the hill, I saw tall ornate gates, the tops of a scroll-like Gothic design. The gates had a translucent quality like pearl. There were no handles, no way I could have opened them. The angel stepped forward and pressed his palms against the gate.

"I stood there for what seemed like a long time, reveling in the wonderful music. The feel of beauty was everywhere. From time to time I would sing along with the voices in the distance. I remember two of the songs—old, old hymns: 'For I Have Been Born Again' and 'The Old Account Was Settled Long Ago.' Finally the angel spoke. 'Would you like to enter and sing with them?'

"I answered, 'No, I would like to stand here and sing awhile, then go back to my family.'

"The angel nodded. I sensed that the choice was mine. Then I was coming back down the grassy slope, and the sun was on my left coming up over the wall. I remember noticing details like the sharp shadow of the beautiful gates on the wall."

It was at that moment that the world of spirit and this world of time and space fused back together for Betty. In her room the sun was also coming up. Under the sheet Betty began to feel the rising sun warming her cold body.

Despite the sheet over her head, Betty saw moving, wavy letters about two inches high go before her like a ticker-tape message on the sunbeams. She has no idea whether she was "seeing" with her spiritual eyes or with her physical eyes. After what she had experienced on the grassy slope, she knew that the one is as real as the other.

"The letters," Betty told me, "seemed composed of translucent ivory, only fluid—moving through the rays of the sun. They stretched all the way from the window, past my bed, on into the room, and read, 'I am the resurrection and the life: he that believeth in me, though he were dead, yet shall he live' (John 11:25, KJV).

"The words were so alive that they pulsated. I knew that I had to touch those living words. When I, by faith, reached up to grasp the words, I pushed the sheet off my face. At that instant the Word literally became life to me. The warmth in the moving letters flowed into my fingers and up my arm. I sat up in bed. I was alive!"

At first Betty did not notice her father standing beside her; she had eyes only for the unearthly light in the room and she began to search for its source. Her first awareness was of the vivid greenness of the grass on the hospital lawn—*So beautiful!* she thought—and of a black man carrying on his shoulder a case of 7-Up into the building. Into Betty's heart welled a great love for that man. Then, at last, she noticed her father by her bed.

He was standing there stunned, too stunned to cry out or to hug her ecstatically or to shed tears of joy. Rather, he was rooted to the spot, struck dumb with awe before the majesty of the working of God Himself.

His second reaction was a consuming curiosity to know what Betty had seen, for most of the experience taking place before his eyes had been veiled from him. "Betty, Betty, tell me. What's been going on? Describe it," he ordered, completely forgetting that his daughter had not spoken in weeks.

Nurses and doctors streamed in and out, asking questions. There had been no breathing, no heartbeat, no blood pressure. Between twenty and thirty minutes had elapsed between the telephone call to Mrs. Perkins and the moment Betty had sat up in bed. Now everybody wanted to see Betty, wanted to hear the story from her own lips. When Betty's own doctor kept shaking his head in disbelief, she would look at him in astonishment. "But I'm alive. I can talk and see and smell and feel. I feel fine. And when do I eat?"

Betty had eaten nothing in almost six weeks. Her digestive organs had already started to disintegrate. Hesitantly the doctor authorized giving her an experimental four ounces of 7-Up over crushed ice.

Betty waited eagerly for the drink. Instead, around noon, a tray was set before her—two pork chops, applesauce, cottage cheese, a square of lemon cake with warm sauce, a pot of tea. Hungrily she ate every morsel, thinking it the most delicious food she had ever tasted.

Shortly after that, a flustered nurse rushed in a mobile unit. "I'm going to have to pump out your stomach. You got the wrong tray."

"Oh, please . . . ," Betty protested as the nurse began uncoiling the tubing. "The food tasted so good. It's staying down fine—just fine." After the nurse left, Betty lay there speculating on God's sense of humor. *(Pork chops for the doctor's first experiment?)*

The next day the doctor closed Betty's door, pulled up a chair, and sat by the bed holding her hand. He spoke softly, his voice kind. "There are some medical facts I must help you face," he began gravely. "You may have a hard life ahead of you. Peritonitis and gangrene have caused a disintegration of the organs of your body. You may have to wear a bag on your side for elimination. In my opinion, you must never try to have another child."

The doctor went on to warn Betty that she had been blind for weeks and should be ready for this to recur. Further, so many heavy narcotics had been administered that there was every likelihood of a severe withdrawal problem.

Betty lay there letting the grim words pour over her, but somehow they didn't penetrate. "I certainly want to be realistic," she told the kind doctor. She had always prided herself on being a down-to-earth person, but now, the knowledge of that other world—so beautiful, so solid, where everything is right, so close at hand—lingered and would not be denied. Deep within her was the assurance that God "hath done all things well" (Mark 7:37, KJV).

Over sixteen years have gone by. Betty never had to wear a bag. Her eyesight has been better than ever.

"And any other baby you have might well be deformed," the doctor had said. Sitting there in the living room at our farm, instinctively Betty's eyes, and mine, went to her delightful daughter April, who was romping in the yard outside. Nothing ethereal or otherworldly about this healthy little girl. Her mother's joy in life is clearly reflected in her.

Great as the physical miracle for Betty Malz is, much greater still are the gifts and graces that have accompanied it. Among them, a new appreciation for life itself, a new love for people. "I had to 'die' to learn how to live," she told me. "God had to take my life away long enough to teach me how to use it. Best of all, now I know there's nothing at all to fear in death. It's simply changing locations.

"Every morning is like Easter. I wake up to the light of day so grateful. Unfailingly the dawn breaks, part of the Light of the world. Just as unfailing is His love and care for each one of us. Now I know—we can trust Him utterly."

Great-Aunt Antoinette's Angels

Carla Wills-Brandon

MY AUNT ANTOINETTE, AT AGE SEVENTY-EIGHT, was in a nursing home at the time, and my sons and I visited regularly. She was particularly close to my youngest son, who was two. Tyler Evan and I began to visit her daily first thing in the morning after my two older sons were off to elementary school.

Our visits continued daily, and eventually the day came when it was very clear the end had come. Aunt Ann was weak but, as usual, was clearly thrilled to see her Tyler who by now was almost three and a half. Tyler was aware she was very, very sick. He had made a very special friend, Ulysses, who was the maintenance man at the nursing facility. Ulysses would take Tyler to the arts and crafts room so he could visit with the other patients while I sat with my aunt. I prayed, sang hymns, held her, and just loved her.

Weakly, she began telling me who was coming to visit her. All were deceased relatives. I encouraged her to look for the light, that the family would guide her home. Three times during the course of several hours she opened her eyes, looked over my shoulders, over my head, and simply said, "Angel." At the time, I thought she meant I was her angel.

She told me she loved me, my prayers continued, her breathing became more labored, her eyes closed. These were the last words she ever spoke, as she never regained consciousness again.

During these hours I spent with her, Ulysses brought Tyler back into the room every half hour or so, so he could see I was still there with his dearly loved great-aunt Antoinette. Eventually, it was time for me to take Tyler home and meet my older sons from school. I had planned on going back to the nursing home after getting the boys settled, but the call came that she had passed gently and quietly.

I had to go to the nursing home to sign the authorization for her body to be transported to the funeral parlor. I was quite sad and cried when I told my boys that Great-Aunt Ann had died. Tyler, my precious boy, threw his arms around me and said, "Mommy, don't cry. Didn't you see the three angels standing behind you waiting to take Great-Aunt Antoinette to heaven?" The grace and peace this gave me was incredible.

He insisted on going to the funeral, insisted he view her body to "be sure she was gone." I was apprehensive but carried him to the casket, and with complete joy, he loudly announced, "Yep, she's gone! See?" He also shared she was at the funeral parlor with the angels. My three-year-old Tyler said Aunt Antoinette was happy and he was not sad, so I shouldn't be either.

A Visitation from an Angel

Carla Wills-Brandon

THE YEAR 1996 WAS A very, very hard year for my family. During this time, my husband, children, and I helped my father-in-law pass. "Da," as my two boys called him, was a six-foot-tall Frenchman who rescued a number of family members from concentration camps after the Holocaust. When he and my mother-in-law came to the States, Da began a successful career as an eye surgeon, while Mom worked as a professor at the local university.

My two sons loved their grandfather. Even after his stroke, which left him bedridden, the boys had no difficulty camping out on his bed, eating popcorn, and watching cartoons. Often, I would have to drag my boys away from Da's bedside. Grandfather and grandsons just had too much fun together.

Several weeks before my father-in-law's passing, my youngest son made an announcement. While traveling to the grocery store, he informed me that there was a "red-haired kid" sitting with him in the backseat of the car. I did a double take in the rearview mirror just to make sure Josh was alone with only his toy dinosaurs. Noting the empty seat beside my son, I decided to play along with what I thought, at the time, was one more three-year-old game.

"Honey, what's your friend's name?" I asked. While pulling at the legs of his dinosaur, Josh looked at the seat beside him and answered, "Who, him? That kid? His name is Damus."

A few days later, while running one more errand, Damus visited us again. Living on an island, we were making our way to a shop situated just across the street from the beach. As I coasted through a stoplight, I asked if Damus was still around. My son looked at me with much irritation, pointed at the seat beside him, and said, "Can't you see him? He is right here!" Once again, I looked in my rearview mirror to make sure I had not unwittingly picked up an unknown passenger. Though I could see nothing, except for my son's stack of plastic, vicious-looking toy creatures, eventually I learned that a third "being" truly was accompanying us from shop to shop.

"Sweetie, how long has Damus been around?" I asked, keeping one eye on the rearview mirror and another on the beachfront street.

"Oh, Damus just got here a few days ago," answered my son as he attacked the backseat with his fanged creature.

"Damus just got here?" I asked. "Is he a friend of yours?"

Still growling away, Josh said, "No, Mom! He just got here! He came here for Da!"

It was Friday the thirteenth. We decided to take a break from the hospital and round up the boys for a family-night service at our temple. Rabbi Jimmy is a wonderful, down-to-earth guy who loves hearing about the mystical experiences of others. I pulled Jimmy aside and asked him if he had ever heard the term "Damus." This was all I shared with him. He suddenly took out a pen and started writing in Aramaic and then Hebrew. After pondering over his writings for a moment, he looked up and said, "Sure, Damus or Damas, depending on the spelling, translates to 'messenger of death.' According to our (Jewish) tradition, the messenger of death or angel of death is a positive being who assists the dying. Where did you hear this term? It isn't that common."

I was speechless! I didn't know what to say. My youngest son had been receiving deathbed visions. Suddenly, I started to cry. Rabbi Jimmy found my response somewhat alarming and asked, "What's up?" While blowing my nose, I shared with him about our strange visitor.

His only response was "Wow!"

My father-in-law gently passed away in my husband's arms on Friday the thirteenth, the day after Hanukkah, right after his favorite TV program, the ten o'clock news. After his death, my young son Josh received no more visitations from Damus.

A Big Fish Came
Ned Dougherty

It was a beautiful summer day when I unlatched a gateway on the protective fence surrounding the pool. I was momentarily distracted moving the pool furniture and organizing things when two-year-old Michael slipped quietly behind me and toddled down the side of the pool to the deepest end. I can still remember that feeling. It was a sickening feeling that came over me as I was moving a chair. Suddenly I was frozen to the spot; I felt as if a part of my soul had been torn away from me. It was one of those moments in life when time and space seem to stand still.

Something was missing! As I turned toward the pool, I watched helplessly as Michael, seemingly in slow motion, stumbled and fell into the deepest end of the pool. I ran and then I dove and swam to the bottom of the pool to the deepest point where Michael's body had quickly sunk. I instinctively knew from lifeguard training that his lungs must have filled with water, as he sank like a stone. As I reached down for his body, I noticed how he seemed to be floating peacefully at the bottom of the pool, his arms and legs extended out strongly but motionless.

As I wrapped my arm around his body and propelled us both to the surface, I applied pressure with my hand beneath his chest cavity and pressed down to remove the water from his body. As we broke the surface, I watched as a stream of water gushed from his mouth.

His face was radiant with an expression as if he had just experienced a wonderful event. When the water was finally purged and he began to breathe heavily, his eyes were beaming and his mouth formed a large *O* shape.

I was amazed at how much strength I mustered at that moment as I held Michael with one arm and lifted us both out of the water with one swift motion of the other arm. I knew that he was okay, but I'll never forget the first words he mumbled: "Daddy! What was that?"

A year and a half later, Michael and I were returning from a US Marine Corps Reserve Center, where we had delivered several truckloads of toys for the Toys for Tots program. On the way home, Michael and I stopped at a roadside stand and bought our Christmas tree. After securing the tree across the roof of the Jeep wagon, I drove east down the highway to our home in the Hamptons. The sun was setting in the west as a full moon rose on the horizon at the end of the highway directly in front of us. It seemed as if we could have driven right up to it. I continued driving, glancing at Michael and watching as the moonbeams bounced off his rosy cheeks.

"Daddy, do you remember when I drowned in the pool?" I was shocked that Michael was recalling this incident. He had not mentioned it before in the year and a half since that day.

"Yes, I remember, Michael, but I am surprised that you remember it."

"Remember, Daddy, I drowned and I died, but did I go to heaven?"

"No, Michael, you didn't die. You fell in the pool, and Daddy jumped in and pulled you out, but you didn't die."

"Yes, I did!" He was adamant. "I drowned, and I died!"

"And then what happened?" I responded, filled with curiosity.

"Well, when I drowned, and I died, a big, big fish came along, and he scooped me up and took me to a big flashlight in the sky."

"No, Michael," I said. "I scooped you up and saved you!" As I spoke, I realized what my son was trying to tell me, and I was denying him his experience.

"No, Daddy." He was very insistent. "I drowned, and I died! And the big, big fish scooped me up and took me to a big, big flashlight!"

I sat silent. Michael was describing his own near-death experience.

We continued to drive in silence. It seemed as if we were driving right to the moon, which was still directly in front of us and brighter and larger than I have ever seen it.

Finally, Michael broke the silence. "Daddy, when I died, I saw Grandpa. You know, the Grandpa Michael." Michael had never seen his Grandpa Michael before, at least not in this world. Grandpa Michael died four years before Michael was born.

Another minute of silence. I was continually glancing at Michael as I drove, observing that he was obviously deep in thought. I knew that this was a special moment between a father and his son that I would remember for eternity.

Michael broke the silence again. "Daddy, isn't God wonderful?"

"He truly is," I responded. "He truly is."

Sweet souls around us watch us still,

press nearer to our side; into our thoughts,

into our prayers, with gentle helpings glide.

—HARRIET BEECHER STOWE

Angels of Christmas

An angel of the Lord appeared to them, and the glory of

the Lord shone around them, and they were terrified. But the angel

said to them, "Do not be afraid. I bring you good news that will

cause great joy for all the people. Today in the town of David

a Savior has been born to you; he is the Messiah, the Lord.

This will be a sign to you: You will find a baby wrapped

in cloths and lying in a manger."

—LUKE 2:9–12 (NIV)

My Angel of Christmas
Peter Gianakura

I ASKED MY WIFE, GEORGIA, to give me some ideas of things she would like for Christmas. She didn't hesitate. "I would be pleased with only one gift," she said. "That you quit smoking."

Anyone addicted to cigarettes knows how difficult it is to quit. Whenever business got slow at the café we owned—or too busy—I eased my nerves with a smoke. Georgia worried about my health, as did I, but I couldn't stay motivated long enough to fight that urge to light up. I tried again, but by Christmas I was still sneaking drags of a cigarette when the cravings became too much to bear. Georgia forgave me, though I knew she was disappointed.

Not long after the holiday, I paced the café one afternoon, trying again to fight that craving. The lunch rush had come and gone; my waitress and I were the only ones there. Perfect time for a smoke. I approached the cigarette vending machine near the entrance, dropped my coins in, and pulled the lever for my brand.

That's when I felt a tap on my shoulder.

Startled, I looked up to see a man with a tan complexion and penetrating blue eyes. He gave me a pleasant smile. "I just want to tell you, as one human being to another, you are killing yourself," he said. Then he gently tapped my shoulder again and left the café.

I asked the waitress if she had served the man. "What man?" she said. "It's just been you and me in here since lunch."

Soon after, I quit smoking for good. I credit the motivation of that mysterious stranger, who helped me give a belated Christmas gift to my wife and added years to my life.

Seaside SOS

Carol Lynn Sikes

EVEN A PLACE AS BEAUTIFUL as St. Simons Island could feel dreary when I was all alone. My husband was working out of town, and I was left to take care of our eleven-month-old son, Edward, by myself.

"Why don't you come with me to Fernandina Beach?" Mom called to ask. "It's never crowded in November. I'm going to do some early Christmas shopping in the area, and you two can frolic in the ocean." Why not? Maybe there'd be other kids to play with. But when Mom dropped us off, the place was deserted.

"Looks like it's just us," I told Edward as I carried him across the warm sand. I put down a blanket, and Edward toddled toward the water, laughing when the tide licked at his toes. He pointed eagerly at the sparkling blue expanse in front of him. "All right," I said, picking Edward up. "Let's take a dip."

Holding my baby securely, I waded out into the surf, careful not to venture in too deep. Edward was delighted with our little adventure and squirmed in my arms. I took another step into the ocean. The sand beneath my feet disappeared! I dropped, flailing into the waves. I struggled to tread water and keep Edward's head above the surface. We were caught in an undertow! Water pulled at us from all sides, creating a whirlpool-like hole that dragged us under. Edward was choking and coughing up water. My son was drowning! I kicked my way to the surface again and again, but I was getting weaker. *God, help us!* I thought frantically.

Hands grasped my arms from behind. The grip was strong but soft at the same time. *What a man this must be,* I thought. The water was no match for him. He lifted Edward and me together, as if we were light as can be. *But this is an odd way to carry us,* I thought. He set us down gently back on our beach blanket. I pushed myself up on to my elbows and shook the salt water from my eyes. I turned to thank our rescuer—but there was no one there. Not a soul in sight. My son and I were all alone.

Edward, crying and spitting up salt water, was lying safely on my stomach. I wrapped him in a towel. Just as I finished calming him, I spotted my mother's car awaiting us past the dunes. Exhausted and relieved, I trudged up to it.

"Look what I found today!" Mom exclaimed before I could tell her what had happened. She opened a brown box. Nestled inside was a Dresden angel, cast in porcelain and coated in a cloud-white glaze. The angel's wings were spread, hands clasped in prayer. Despite being made of porcelain, those hands somehow looked gentle and soft, just like the hands that had swept us from the ocean. "What is it?" Mom said, suddenly noticing my distress.

"We had quite a scare," I started. I grasped the figurine as Edward batted playfully at its wings. I felt the chill of the ocean melting away, warmed by a sun that was reflecting off the ivory glaze. Even if I sometimes felt lonely, I now knew I was never truly alone.

A Giant beside Our House

Ron Gullion

I'M IN OUR YARD on Big Fir Court, gazing up at the mighty 250-foot tree the street is named for. Rising from the corner of our property to the height of a twenty-story building, the great white fir dwarfs our home and everything in sight like some ancient giant. It gives the illusion of leaning ominously toward me, creaking and swaying ever so slightly in the rustling wind.

Look! It's not leaning, it's falling! It's toppling toward our house, gaining momentum, rushing to meet its shadow, until finally it crumples the roof and splinters through the living room and front bedroom with a sickening, thunderous roar. I let out a cry. Alison's room!

I awoke in a drenching sweat and sat straight up trying to blink away the terrifying vision. Another nightmare. I slipped out of bed and stole a peek into Alison's room. Our nine-year-old daughter was sleeping peacefully, as was eleven-year-old Heath across the hall. But I couldn't shake the irrational fear until I'd checked. This was not the first time I'd dreamed of such an accident. In another dream I'd seen a giant tree limb tearing loose and slamming down on Heath, leaving him crippled.

As a computer engineer, I deal with quantifiable information. I don't pay much attention to impractical things like dreams. But these nightmares were so vivid and frightening. I eased back into bed next to my wife, Nita, but not before looking out the window at the tree. There it stood, stately and still, its coarse bark ghostly pale in the faint moonlight.

A few nights later I had another dream, this one more puzzling than alarming:

I am in our yard and in front of me stands a white angel. The angel has a broken wing.

What did all these dreams mean?

Then one day I noticed a twenty-foot dead limb dangling from the fir. Out here in the Northwest we call a dangerous limb like that a widow maker. I remembered the dream about Heath. "Don't go near that tree," I warned him. That Saturday I enlisted a neighbor to help me rope it down; all week I'd worried about the precarious branch. Later I had some other dead limbs removed too.

Why am I so concerned about this tree? I wondered. *It's stood here for genera-tions. It even survived the fierce Columbus Day storm of 1962.*

My nightmares about the tree eventually subsided. Christmas season arrived and Nita and I rushed madly to get our shopping done. More than anything, Alison wanted a Cabbage Patch doll. We scoured the stores around Portland with no luck. Everywhere we went it was the same story. "Sorry, folks," said the clerk inevitably. "We sold out our Cabbage Patch dolls weeks ago."

Finally Nita settled on a handmade rag doll. It was thicker and heavier than the Cabbage Patch version, but there was something about it that caught our fancy. "Well," sighed Nita as we paid for it, "this will have to do."

"Alison will love it," I reassured her.

We arrived home to a surprise. Alison had impetuously decided to rearrange her room. She'd been talking about it for days, but Nita had implored her to wait until the holiday excitement died down. "Then I'll help you," she'd promised.

Instead Alison had recruited her brother for the task, getting Heath to help drag her heavy bed across the room. "I just wanted to get it done now, Mommy," she explained as Nita surveyed the scene with obvious displeasure. "It's important." Alison's toys and furniture spilled out into the hall. By bedtime, however, Alison had her room in order again and we could scarcely hide our admiration.

"See?" said Alison knowingly. "It's not such a big deal."

Outside I heard the wind whistle through the big fir.

A howling blizzard marked Christmas Eve. I drove home from work through swirling snow and pounding winds. I pulled into the driveway, turned up my collar, and hurried inside to get ready for church. Church was not one of my priorities even under the best circumstances, and on a night like this I didn't want to be anywhere but inside my house, Christmas Eve or not. But I'd promised.

At the service with Nita and the kids, I felt strangely detached as I hunched in the pew with my arms folded tightly, thinking about whether I even believed that God was a part of my life. I'd been raised in church but that was a long time ago. Now I certainly didn't feel any "tidings of comfort and joy." God may have created the world and all its wonders, but I didn't see where that had much to do with my life. If God was real, He was much too remote for me to have faith in.

We arrived home late, and the wind and snow stung our faces as we walked up the driveway. Heath and Alison rushed inside to turn on the Christmas tree lights. From our bay window the blue lights cast a peaceful glow across the snowy yard. I draped my arm around Nita and led her in.

Wrapping paper flew as the children tore into their presents, and Nita and I settled back on the couch to view the happy chaos. Nita had turned the tree into a work of art. The crowning touch was a glorious blonde angel perched high at the top. "It looks like Alison," I said.

Alison was so delighted with her big new doll that she granted it the honor of accompanying her to bed. "Told you she'd love it," I reminded Nita as we climbed under the covers. The moaning wind lulled us to sleep.

ROAR! The explosive sound jolted the house. I hadn't been asleep long, and my startled, half-awake mind tried to separate fantasy from reality. *The dream again,* I thought. But then I sat bolt upright, and suddenly I knew. This was no dream. This time my nightmare was real. The tree really had fallen on our house!

I leaped out of bed and raced across the hall to Alison's room. "Daddy, help!" she was calling frantically. "I'm stuck!"

I couldn't budge the door. It was jammed shut. "Oh, my God," I whispered. "Don't move, honey!" I shouted through the door. "We'll get you out." I grabbed a flashlight and told Nita to call 911. "I'll see if I can get to her from outside."

I was horrified to find the tree filling the front hall, branches whipping in the gale. I stumbled through the family room to a side door. Outside I nearly collided with the massive trunk. Propped up on its giant ball of roots, which had been torn from the earth, it looked prehistoric. I crawled underneath as the rough bark tore at my robe and ripped my flesh. The wind sliced through me. Above the din I heard the distant wail of sirens.

Groping my way to Alison's window, I aimed the flashlight beam inside and wiped the icy snow from my eyes. All I could see were branches, tattered insulation, and hunks of ceiling strewn about the trunk. Somewhere buried beneath the tree was my daughter, crying faintly, "Daddy! Daddy!"

Someone was standing beside me. "Alison! This is Captain McCullough of the fire department," he called. "Your daddy's with me. Can you move at all?"

"I think I can move my arm," came a brave little voice.

"Good. Push your hand up as high as you can."

Tiny fingers wriggled up through the debris. I breathed a tentative sigh of relief. Firemen rushed to set up lights and heat lamps. They fastened a plastic tarp over the rescue area. Captain McCullough turned to me and said quietly, "This isn't going to be easy, Mr. Gullion."

As I huddled with Nita, and neighbors looked after Heath, a terrifying game of pick-up-sticks slowly unfolded. The night air was filled with the roar of chain saws and the reek of fir pitch as rescuers cut away at the tree and cautiously removed branches as they went. A slight shift of any debris could spell disaster.

Bit by bit they chipped away at the wreckage until, after an hour, Alison's head and shoulders emerged. Her right leg appeared to be crushed under the tree. A fallen two-by-six rafter clamped down on her torso. We could see Alison's new doll squeezed between her chest and the rafter. Apparently she'd fallen asleep clutching it.

McCullough shook his head grimly and called a halt to the work. "We can't risk it," he said. "Show me the crawl space." Moments later he played his flashlight on the area under Alison's room. Limbs a half foot in diameter pierced the floor and stabbed the ground beneath. Again McCullough shook his head. "We can't cut away the floor without disturbing the tree. And that tree must not shift."

The subzero wind had intensified. Hours had passed and now there was the threat of Alison succumbing to hypothermia. Neighbors rushed in warm blankets and hot-water bottles. A paramedic put his wool ski cap on Alison's head. But I could see she was drifting, her big eyes fluttering. Once or twice her head rolled back. If we didn't get her leg out soon, the surgeons might have to amputate it to free her.

Only one chance was left: Lift the tree. A crane was out of the question. In this wind it would be too unstable. But McCullough had called a towing company that used giant air bags to gently right overturned semitrailers. "It's a gamble," he warned me. "But we've run out of options."

Huge rubber bags were packed under the tree. A compressor roared to life. Slowly the bags filled with air and swelled against the great fir. Despite the blizzard, I could see sweat bead up on McCullough's tensed brow. My hands trembled as Nita buried her head in my chest, afraid to look.

Suddenly I heard myself praying to the God whose very existence, just hours earlier, I'd doubted. You would have thought I'd be ashamed to ask His help now, but something told me I must. "Please, Lord," I begged, "spare her life. I believe You are there."

The shriek of the compressor was deafening. The bags bulged like great pillows, but at first nothing gave.

Then there was movement! Inch by agonizing inch, the tree was lifted. A cry rose from the crowd as paramedics rushed to free Alison and whisk her to a waiting ambulance. Nita and I jumped in with her, and we roared off. Alison smiled weakly. "I'll be okay now, Daddy," she whispered, still grasping her new doll.

That overstuffed doll, it turned out, was possibly just enough of a cushion between the fallen two-by-six rafter and Alison's chest to have saved her life.

The doctors confirmed that she would recover. And Alison's leg was only broken, not crushed.

Christmas Day, Heath and I kicked through the rubble of our house. I'd been thinking about that desperate prayer I'd said, thinking about it a lot. In Alison's room I saw that the bulk of the fir had landed near the southeast wall—right where her bed had been before she'd impulsively moved it. On the trunk directly over where Alison lay when the tree came crashing through, I noticed a wide scar from a recently cut branch—one of those I'd felt such urgency to remove after my dream. That branch might have killed her.

Had God been trying to warn me all along about the tree? To protect us? Had I been blind to God's ways?

In the snow outside what used to be our living room I found the angel from our Christmas tree, the one that looked like Alison. Its wing was broken, just as the angel's wing in my dream had been. As I brushed it off and held it up, Heath came running. "Dad, Dad!" He grabbed the angel. "I've seen this before! In a dream! An angel with a broken wing just like this one!"

Dreams. Does God speak to us through them? The Bible says He does, Job 33:14–18 as well as in many other ways. This much I myself can say: Alison is safe and well. And God is, and always has been, watching over my family.

In Need of Repair

Pamela Jones

ICY SLUSH COVERED ONTARIO'S HIGHWAY 401. The white lines separating lanes were completely hidden, and our windshield wipers struggled to keep up with the dirty chunks of brown snow that the road spit up. Blinking orange signs warned: DRIVE WITH CAUTION. "And we figured we were playing it safe by taking the highway," my husband said. But surely the back roads were worse. What a post-Christmas letdown.

Martin and I liked picturesque scenery and quaint country lanes. On car trips we tried to spend at least one night at a cozy inn, or stop for dinner at an out-of-the-way restaurant. The drive home to Toronto from my daughter's house in Ottawa was only five hours, but when we took our time we always experienced something new and exciting along the way. This storm had other plans for us.

Screech! An ominous scraping sound came from underneath the car. "What's that?" I asked.

"Who knows," Martin said. It was enough to crush what was left of our Christmas spirit.

We slowed to a crawl until an exit appeared, then pulled into the parking lot of a fast-food place. As soon as we got out of the car, the problem was obvious: part of the rear bumper had detached and was dragging. What now? "Let's get a cup of coffee," Martin suggested. We settled into a booth to consider our options. "Look," Martin said, pointing out the window. "There's an auto-repair place right across the street." We finished our coffee and drove over, with the bumper loudly dragging behind in protest.

A woman greeted us inside. Auburn curls were piled on top of her head, and she smiled so warmly at us she reminded me of a hostess at one of the bed-and-breakfasts Martin and I sometimes liked to spend the night at. "I guess you've come about that bumper," she said, a twinkle in her brown eyes.

It was a busy place. I was surprised that she'd been at the door to greet us, and even more surprised that she noticed our bumper. She walked us over to the service counter. "I'm sorry," the receptionist said, "all our mechanics have their hands full."

Martin and I stepped away from the counter to regroup. The woman who had greeted us had a word with the receptionist, then turned to us. "A spot opened up," she announced.

We took a seat in the waiting room and our greeter appeared again. "My son Jeremy will service your car himself," she said.

In time, a young mechanic with the name tag "Jeremy" and familiar brown eyes came into the waiting room. "I was able to fix the bumper enough to get you back to Toronto," he said. "But when you get home you'll have to take it in for further repairs." Mike and I were beaming as we walked out of the shop. Christmas was over on the calendar, but the Christmas spirit was alive and well in this place.

A few months later I decided to take another quick trip to see my daughter. I took the highway so I could stop in at the auto-repair shop and say hi. The place was as busy as it had been when we were so desperate for help. But this time my greeter and her son were nowhere to be found. I went to the service counter and asked for Jeremy.

"There's no one here by that name," the receptionist said.

"He fixed my car at Christmastime," I said. "His mother worked here too. She had auburn hair."

"I'm sorry," the receptionist said. "We haven't had any staff changes since Christmas, and no one here fits your description."

Mike and I didn't expect to see anything exciting when we took the highway that Christmas. But it was our best car trip yet—the one where we met two angels.

Ten Precious Minutes

Nelson Sousa

ON DECEMBER 19, 1979, my partner Ray and I were working as construction divers at a bridge site near Somers Point, New Jersey. Snow had begun to fall early, and by noon it had gotten so heavy we had to knock off work.

As we waded through parking-lot drifts, I noticed that my boss's car didn't have snow tires.

"Hey, John," I said to him, "why don't you let me drive you home? I don't think you'll make it with those tires."

John considered for a moment, then nodded. "Okay, Nelson, you might be right." But as he started toward my pickup, he stopped and turned back to his car. "Oh, I almost forgot," he said, reaching into its trunk. "Here's your spare dry suit I borrowed last month. I finally remembered to bring it back."

I was about to take the suit to our onsite trailer office where we store gear. But since it had some holes in it, I decided to take it home to repair. I threw it into the back of my pickup. It was the first time in my ten years of diving that I had traveled anywhere with one of these protective rubber suits. They were always stored at work.

The drive north through the snow was rough; stop-and-go all the way. What should have taken us one hour took over three. But we spent time talking about Christmas and the toys we were buying our kids.

I didn't really mind going out of the way for John, but by the time we got to his turnoff it was past three o'clock. We turned into his street. A fire engine roared by and stopped at the end of the block. There was a big commotion down there.

"Oh, dear God, no . . . ," John said. Ahead was an alarming tableau: a frozen pond, an ominous black hole in its center. Firetrucks with lights flashing and people crowding the bank. A woman squalling and weeping.

"Somebody must have fallen through the ice," Ray said.

I pulled the pickup over to the side, jumped out, grabbed my dry suit from the back, pulled it on, and ran to the pond. Ray stumbled along behind me zipping me up.

A grim-faced firefighter told us that a six-year-old boy had walked out on the ice and fallen in. "But it's hopeless," he groaned, "the ice is too thin for us to get out there." Two men had already tried. Even a ladder laid on the ice didn't work. And the water was so cold that anyone falling into it would be shocked into unconsciousness in minutes.

"I'll try," I said. Someone tied a rope around my waist and I headed out, splintering the ice into shards as I beat my way through it. By the time I reached the hole where the boy had disappeared, my hands were bleeding from the exertion.

Icy water surged through the holes in the suit I was going to repair. I knew I had only a minute or two for a dive. Then I discovered I had left my heavy diver's belt back at the job. Without it to weigh me down, it would be hard to swim underwater in my buoyant rubber suit. But I had to get down to the bottom.

All I could do was force my body down. The water looked black. About six feet down I touched the bottom, then bobbed up like a cork. Up and down, up and down I plunged, working partway around the opening in the ice frantically feeling for a body. But there was nothing, only frigid water and a slick muddy bottom. Where was he?

Gasping, coughing from exhaustion, I cried out in desperation: "He's not here! I can't find him. Where is he?"

Looking up across the pond, I saw a tall blond man in a light jacket standing by himself in the snow. He raised his arm and pointed to a spot on the side of the hole opposite me.

I pushed to the spot and thrust myself down. The ice-cold water closed over my head, and then my foot touched something. The boy's body! I surged up again. Now, with violent arm movements, I forced myself down and wrapped my feet around the body and drew it up. Floating on my back, I pulled the limp, sodden form across my chest and held him tight.

The little boy's soaked blue jacket seemed glued to him. I pulled back the hood covering his head and screamed. The pinched face was as blue as the jacket. He was not breathing. I could not look at him anymore.

"Pull me back!" I yelled, and the rope tightened around me as firefighters heaved on it, hauling me to the bank. John jumped into the water, took the form, and passed it to waiting medics. I staggered upright, untied the rope, and headed toward them when two policemen grabbed me. "C'mon," one urged, "get into our squad car and warm up."

"But the boy!" I yelled. By now the ambulance's doors had slammed shut and it sped away, siren wailing. I stood shaking my head, feeling helpless, wishing I could have saved him.

John, my boss, took me to his house where I warmed up some more and then Ray and I drove home. When I walked in, my wife, Patricia, was preparing dinner. I didn't even kiss her, just stumbled over to the sofa and slumped down sobbing. It had all been so useless.

Pat looked at Ray. "Nelson pulled a little boy out of the pond," Ray explained.

Patricia had cooked my favorite dish, beef stroganoff, but I couldn't touch it. I could only sit on the living room sofa thinking about that poor little fellow and how his parents were feeling.

Patricia called the hospital where the boy had been taken. They told her that little Michael Polukard had been underwater for around ten minutes. He was unconscious, in serious condition; a priest had given him last rites, but he was alive.

What a Christmas, I thought, staring into the glowing lights on our tree. Under it was our Nativity scene; the manger bed was empty—our custom is to place the Baby Jesus in it on Christmas Eve. I felt even worse thinking about a real little bed that was empty that night.

I looked gloomily around the room. On the TV set stood two white angels Patricia had made for the house that year. One held a string of stars, the other played a harp. How frivolous it all seemed now. Angels! I remembered how my Portuguese grandmother used to tell us kids about the angels who sang of Jesus's birth to the shepherds that long-ago night. But that night angels and Jesus didn't seem very real to me. And yet, my heart grieved so for the little boy that I did the only thing left for me to do. I leaned my head down and prayed for him. I asked God to help him live.

Hours passed as I sat, moodily staring at the wall. Patricia put our two little girls to bed and Ray tried to encourage me. "He's still alive, you know," Ray said. "There's hope. You should just be grateful that you knew where to find him in that pond."

I looked up. "I didn't know where he was, Ray," I said. "It was that big blond guy who pointed me to the right spot. If it hadn't been for him, I never would have found the boy."

Ray looked puzzled. "That's the strangest thing, Nelson. You keep talking about some guy on the other side of the pond but"—he scratched his head—"there wasn't anybody over there."

About nine o'clock the phone rang. Patricia took it, then handed it to me. "It's Michael's father, he wants to thank you."

With shaking hand, I took the phone. "Don't worry about me," I blurted, "all I want to know is how your little boy is."

Stan Polukard said Michael was still in serious condition, but it looked as though he was going to make it. The very coldness of the water had slowed Michael's body functions, he explained, reducing his need for oxygen. I gave a big sigh of relief and, in my heart, thanked God for saving the little boy. Then I was able to fall into bed and sleep.

We kept in close touch with the hospital the following days, but the news wasn't good. The Polukards had been warned that Michael might have extensive brain damage. The doctors worried about all the time that had passed before his heart and lungs had resumed functioning. A test of his brain by an electroencephalogram had shown "inconclusive" results. Doctors said that only after he regained consciousness would they know how much he'd been damaged.

We learned that his mother and father had moved into the hospital to stay with the boy. The news reported that they were praying for him around the clock. People everywhere sent encouraging messages, saying they were praying with them. I didn't know that there were that many strong believers.

The papers kept up a running account of Michael's plight. Eileen and Stan Polukard continued to talk to their little boy, who lay unconscious, connected to a respirator, a heart monitor, and intravenous lines. The doctors tried to protect them from false hope.

"Remember," one doctor warned Eileen, "the child you knew may no longer exist."

On the third day, Friday, the medical staff took Michael off the respirator. Stan and Eileen continued their patient, prayerful vigil at their son's bedside. Suddenly, Michael began to stir. Then, opening his eyes, he slowly turned toward them. "Hi, Mom, hi, Dad," he whispered.

On Monday afternoon, Christmas Eve, we got a phone call.

"Michael's home!" my wife shouted. The Polukards had called saying that tests showed Michael completely well and normal and that they could take him home. They invited us to their house to celebrate with them.

Patricia and I bundled our two little girls into the car and hurried over.

Michael was dressed in pajamas and sitting on the living room sofa when we came in. "Do you know who I am?" I asked. For the rest of the evening he wouldn't leave my side. And as we talked he happened to mention that one of the first things he saw when he opened his eyes in the hospital was an angel.

"An angel?" I said, surprised.

There had been an angel there, all right. A big paper angel had hung over Michael's bed as part of the hospital's Christmas decorations.

Angels again. Once more I thought of that mysterious time my grandmother used to tell us about when the angels spoke to the shepherds in the fields and told them about the little Baby lying in a manger.

I pictured our own little crèche in our living room at home. When we'd get back, our two little girls would place the Baby Jesus in His manger bed.

I glanced up and saw Michael in his father's arms and I gave thanks to the One Who had sent us His Son . . . and Who, I now knew for certain, sent His help, somehow, someway, so that another little bed would be warm tonight.

But there was another picture in my mind, a tall blond man standing alone in the snow beside the pond, pointing. Who was he? In all the weeks and months to come, I would find no one who had seen him there. On this happy Christmas Eve, in a room filled with quiet celebration, I couldn't help but wonder.

My Mr. Fix-It
Virginia Mallory

I MISSED MY HUSBAND, MELVIN, every day, but never more than while I prepared for my first Christmas without him. When the light in our angel tree topper went out, it was the last straw. If Melvin were alive, he could have fixed that angel, no problem. He could fix anything. One of my sons-in-law got a ladder and examined the angel from all sides, jiggled her, then wondered if the problem was with the bulb inside. "It's useless," he said finally. "I can't get it out to replace it."

Maybe it's a sign, I thought. *We should be grieving this Christmas instead of celebrating.* We left the unlit angel on top of the tree.

On Christmas Eve my family gathered to watch midnight mass on TV. I felt so low, I could hardly concentrate on the service. At one point, we all bowed our heads to pray. When I looked up again at the priest on TV, I caught sight of our tree topper. The angel lit up right in front of my eyes! Everyone shouted and clapped before settling down to watch the end of the mass in the heavenly glow of the angel's light. It was definitely time to celebrate.

A Host of Christmas Angels

Helen Walker

FRIGID WIND STUNG MY CHEEKS as I walked up the steps to Chicago's St. Hyacinth Basilica near my hometown of Evanston, Illinois. I barely felt the cold. My head was still spinning from the news. I steadied myself on the icy railing. December 7, 1941. I was sixteen years old. I knew I'd never forget this day as long as I lived. *How could it have happened?*

Less than an hour ago my family had been cozy at home, enjoying Sunday dinner. We were all dressed up, my little sister in shiny patent-leather shoes and my four older brothers looking smart in matching ties. Right after the meal we would head over to St. Hyacinth, where Evanston Township High School was hosting its annual Christmas concert for the community.

Our school was known for its musical program, and I was honored to be one of the singers in the chorus. I couldn't wait to perform. We'd been rehearsing for weeks. I knew every note. Singing was my passion and my refuge. My mother said singing was like praying twice. I intended to send my prayers soaring up to heaven at the concert this evening!

Then, while we were finishing up our meal, the phone rang. My father left the table to answer it. "Hello?" he said. "Yes, I'm listening." His eyes widened, and he fell silent. He hung up and turned back to us. "The president just made a radio announcement," he said. "Japan has bombed Pearl Harbor."

The dinner table went quiet. Everyone seemed to hold their breath, unsure of what to do. According to my father, details were still trickling in from the White House. But a few things were already clear—American military person-nel had been caught completely by surprise and thousands on the island naval base had died.

The radio broadcasters warned that nothing could be gained from hysteria, but my mind was jumbled and I felt dizzy. I could see the same shock reflected back at me in the faces of my brothers and sisters, my mother and father. I knew we were sharing the same thought: *How could this have happened? How can this be real?*

My mother's voice finally broke the silence. "Helen, sweetheart, get your coat. We don't want to be late for your concert."

I did as Mother said, and the family drove to the church in silence. All of my excitement had vanished. Worry and doubt crowded my head. Would the United States now enter the war? What would that mean for my big brothers?

An icy chill went through me at the thought, and I pulled my hand from the church railing. For now I had to concentrate on the concert. My mother hurried me up the rest of the stairs. I quickly put away my coat and found my place in the chorus on stage. I looked out at all of the people in the audience. Were they afraid too? How would the war affect them all? My brothers, my family, my community, my country—would we ever be or feel safe again?

Before the program began, one of the teachers from the music depart-ment came to the head of the audience and repeated President Roosevelt's announcement for the crowd. I felt sick. How could any of us be expected to perform?

The orchestra struck the first notes, and my classmates began to sing. I tried to lose myself in the music, but I couldn't push away my anxieties. I looked up at the grand dome of the basilica, praying silently for strength. *Singing is like praying twice*, I told myself.

I mouthed the words to the music, but it was as if I had no voice to sing with. I kept my eyes focused on the dome, its exquisite mural of saints and angels stretching around the base. Bright clouds floated above them, fading into a sky-blue backdrop that led up to a stained-glass window in the center, patterned in azure and gold.

Music filled my ears—orchestral instruments, the voices of my friends. I felt like I was part of a celestial concert. The dome appeared suddenly to me like the inside of some observatory, opening up to reveal the heavens. Glittering stars and rainbow galaxies burst into life, casting colors across the walls of the church. A glorious white-gold staircase shimmered into view, spiraling down from the infinite beyond. On its steps descended a host of angels, their faces bright and joyous. They danced up and down the stairs, their divine song joining our chorus. I realized I was singing too. As our song came to a close, the ceiling above solidified again. The vision vanished. But I was left with a peace I couldn't have expected... especially now.

Maybe it was my imagination, I thought. But deep down inside I knew I had never seen anything so real. When I closed my eyes, I could picture my vision—vividly—once again. And how could something I imagined take away my fear so completely? I no longer had trouble joining in with the choir. I lifted my voice up to God and sang with all my heart. Now I knew that I was singing with the angels.

After the concert I rushed around to my friends in the chorus, asking if they had seen the angels too, or the staircase or perhaps anything unusual at all. I asked my parents, my brothers, and my sisters. They all shook their heads.

Why the heavenly vision was for me alone, I cannot say. But as we sang, I believe I saw Christmas angels carrying our prayers up to God and carrying God's blessings back down on all of us.

A Note from the Editors

WE HOPE YOU ENJOY *The Best Angel Stories 2015*, created by the Books and Inspirational Media Division of Guideposts, a nonprofit organization that touches millions of lives every day through products and services that inspire, encourage, help you grow in your faith, and celebrate God's love in every aspect of your daily life.

Thank you for making a difference with your purchase of this book, which helps fund our many outreach programs to military personnel, prisons, hospitals, nursing homes, and educational institutions. To learn more, visit GuidepostsFoundation.org.

We also maintain many useful and uplifting online resources. Visit Guideposts .org to read true stories of hope and inspiration, access OurPrayer network, sign up for free newsletters, download free e-books, join our Facebook community, and follow our stimulating blogs.

To learn about other Guideposts publications, including the best-selling devotional *Daily Guideposts*, go to ShopGuideposts.org, call (800) 932-2145, or write to Guideposts, PO Box 5815, Harlan, Iowa 51593.

Explore More from
Angels on Earth

FREE *Angel Sightings* eBook

If you love angels, you'll love our FREE *Angel Sightings* eBook filled with stories hand-selected by the editors of *Angels on Earth*. You'll enjoy inspiring, real-life stories of heavenly angels and earthly angels who help people in need.

Get your FREE *Angel Sightings* eBook today at AngelsonEarth.com/ebook

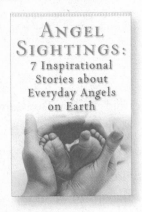

ANGEL
SIGHTINGS:
7 Inspirational
Stories about
Everyday Angels
on Earth

Find *Angels on Earth* on Facebook, Pinterest and Tumblr

Sign up for *Angels on Earth* weekly newsletter at Guideposts.org/newsletters

A Note from the Editors

WE HOPE YOU ENJOY *The Best Angel Stories 2015*, created by the Books and Inspirational Media Division of Guideposts, a nonprofit organization that touches millions of lives every day through products and services that inspire, encourage, help you grow in your faith, and celebrate God's love in every aspect of your daily life.

Thank you for making a difference with your purchase of this book, which helps fund our many outreach programs to military personnel, prisons, hospitals, nursing homes, and educational institutions. To learn more, visit GuidepostsFoundation.org.

We also maintain many useful and uplifting online resources. Visit Guideposts .org to read true stories of hope and inspiration, access OurPrayer network, sign up for free newsletters, download free e-books, join our Facebook community, and follow our stimulating blogs.

To learn about other Guideposts publications, including the best-selling devotional *Daily Guideposts*, go to ShopGuideposts.org, call (800) 932-2145, or write to Guideposts, PO Box 5815, Harlan, Iowa 51593.

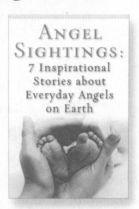